the BIBLE
DIMENSIONS, AND THE SPIRITUAL REALM

ARE HEAVEN, ANGELS, AND GOD CLOSER THAN WE THINK?

JEFF RHOADES Ph. D.

ISBN 978-1-7347170-0-6

Wellingbooks.com
wellingbooks@gmail.com

Cover design and typesetting by MiblArt

CONTENTS

Introduction

Growing up in Missouri, I was well acquainted with the story of the Joplin Spook Light, also known as the Hornet Spook Light. People have been enthralled and captivated with the appearance of this mysterious light ever since it was first reported in the 1800s. Stories are told of a light that randomly appears and mysteriously bobs along a dirt road in northeast Oklahoma just outside Joplin, Missouri. In fact, Joplin's official website has a page devoted to the Spook Light which relates the following about what the website refers to as a paranormal enigma: "Described most often as an orange ball of light, the orb travels from east to west along a four-mile gravel road, long called the Devil's Promenade by area locals."[1] Locals and visitors alike line up along the dirt road waiting to see the mysterious light come traveling down the road, and the web article describes what these spectators have seen with their own eyes. "The ball of fire, described as varying from the size of a baseball to a basketball, dances and spins down the center of the road at high speeds, rising and hovering above the treetops before it retreats and disappears."[2] Is this a supernatural light with a paranormal origin? Experts have studied the aberration without coming to any conclusion. "Though many paranormal and scientific investigators have studied the light, including the Army Corps of Engineers, no one has been able to provide a conclusive answer as to the origin of the light."[3] I never saw the light come bouncing by with my own eyes, but I heard stories of it passing through cars and even down the middle of a bus full of spectators. Many, if not most, of the stories have been grossly exaggerated over time. Though a natural explanation for the phenomenon probably exists, people love to think beyond the physical realm. It seems that we would rather find a paranormal meaning than a physical explanation.

Man is captivated by the supernatural. Fascination with the spiritual, the mystical, and the paranormal in the United States continues to grow. Whether it is biblical beings, like angels or demons, or secularly fictitious beings, like ghosts or the spirits of the dead, people are interested and believe in the unseen world. Hollywood has fed this spiritual fascination with various movies and shows from science fiction adventures to the occult, vampires, the demonic, and the mystical. In his book, *Supernatural*, Michael Heiser writes:

> **Thousands of books, television shows, and movies in the past decade have been about angels, aliens, monsters, demons, ghosts, witches, magic, vampires, werewolves, and superheroes. Many of Hollywood's blockbuster franchises feature the supernatural: The *X-Men*, the *Avengers*, the Harry Potter series, *Superman*, and the *Twilight* saga.**[4]

People, religious or not, are attracted to the spiritual, unseen realm. The allure of the spiritually dark, satanic, evil realm seems to be growing at an alarming rate. Belief in the spiritual world of demons and demon possession goes back thousands of years. Mike Mariani, in an article for *The Atlantic*, writes, "In ancient Mesopotamia, Babylonian priests performed exorcisms by casting wax figurines of demons into a fire... For the ancient Greeks, too, demon-like creatures lurked on the shadowy fringes of the human world."[5] The dark side of the spiritual realm is becoming more and more appealing to and accepted as real by our current society. Whether it is an escape from reality for people through television or movies or something deeper and more spiritual, a belief in the spirit world clearly exists.

The allure that draws the non-religious towards the dark spirit world has begun to make its way into mainstream Christian circles. Mariani writes, "Father Vincent Lampert, the official exorcist for the Archdiocese of Indianapolis, told me in early October that he'd received 1,700 phone or email requests for exorcisms in 2018, by far the most he's ever gotten in one year."[6] Are there really more demon possessions today, or has the plethora of shows, books and movies stoked the fire of belief in demonic possession? Whatever the answer, more professing Christians than ever are expressing a profound belief in the supernatural, and especially the demonic.

People who are religious have always believed in the spiritual realm—though they might not always have a biblically correct view of it. In an article from *The Atlantic*, religion writer Emma Green explains that demon possession and the exorcism of spirits are part of Christianity, Hinduism and Islam. In fact, the spiritual realm is fundamental to Christianity. Green writes, "The Bible has stories of angels speaking to Abraham, Jacob, and David; in Genesis, creatures called Nephilim walk the earth. Many Roman Catholics and Orthodox Christians pray for saints to intervene in their lives. The Vatican routinely reviews miracles claimed to be caused by the holy figures of the

Church."[7] Though the dark side of the spiritual realm receives much of the attention, the spiritual realm is much more than demons and people being possessed. All religions that point to some sort of afterlife believe in a spiritual realm of some kind. No matter the belief system for a religion, the spiritual dimension usually is a central part of their beliefs. The spiritual realm entails angels, God or a supreme being, heaven, hell, miracles, healings, etc. Much, if not most, of the world possesses the clear belief that something more than the physical and material world exists.

Science is the one important and influential institution that has resisted the spiritual dimension and claimed to believe in only what is experienced by the five senses. Science has led to what is called reductionism. Reductionism is believing only in the physical world and universe, and that nothing exists beyond the present world people live in. Bernard Haisch in his book, *The God Theory*, explains reductionism as reducing complex things or processes to the simplest of actions and parts—including humanity and its processes and parts. Haisch writes, "To them [scientists], consciousness is nothing more than brain chemistry. When the ultimate equation has explained the tiniest particle, they claim the job of science will be complete. In their view, there is nothing beyond the here and now; when your body dies, you are gone forever."[8] However, everything changed in the world of science when scientists attempted to unify the forces of gravity and electromagnetism. In the search for the great unifying theory, the theory of everything, science opened the possibility for higher dimensions. The quantum world was not moving towards reductionism. It was bringing new insight and understanding to the physical world. In fact, the more scientists learned about atoms, particles, gravity and the speed of light, the more abstract and intriguing became their theories and views of the universe. String theory came on the scene and took the scientific and non-scientific world alike by storm. String theory introduces a captivating theory involving ten dimensions of space and one dimension of time. This opened the door for the possibilities of seeing the spiritual realm or spiritual dimension in a scientific light without receiving such dismissive remarks and attitudes from the scientific community.

This book seeks to discover where there may be unity between science and the Bible concerning the spiritual realm. By looking at what the Bible has taught for thousands of years in light of what scientists have uncovered in the last few hundred years, one can understand the spiritual dimensions in the Scriptures from a different perspective. Is the spiritual realm not so far out and crazy after all? How does seeing the spiritual dimension in a scientific light bring clearer understanding to heaven, God, angels and time?

This book will show the evidence from the Word of God and from the world of science that confirm the reality of a spiritual dimension or dimensions. The spiritual realm will be explored by looking through a biblical lens while examining the discoveries in science that agree with the Word of God. The first chapter of this book will lay the foundation for the reality of the spiritual realm from the Word of God. The Bible begins with the assumption of the spiritual realm, spiritual dimension, or higher dimension (all three are used interchangeably in this book). Throughout the Word of God, events are taking place that make sense only when understood in light of spiritual dimensions. Creation, angels coming to earth and going to heaven, miracles of various sorts, the incarnation of Jesus Christ, the resurrection of Jesus Christ, and the coming of the Holy Spirit to dwell in believers are all understood better by understanding the spiritual realm.

Next, the foundation for higher dimensions will be laid down from a basic scientific understanding. Geometry and the concept of more spatial dimensions as well as string theory and the possibility for up to ten spatial dimensions will both be considered. Science reveals that people, the universe, and everything in it is digital and made up of small building blocks called atoms and molecules. In subsequent chapters, questions such as the following will be addressed: Did a grand designer create the universe and people? Is the universe much like a digital computer-simulated reality that was created and somehow maintained by a grand programmer? Did humanity bring a virus called sin into the digitally simulated reality? Did the grand programmer enter into the digitally simulated reality as the fully God, fully man Jesus Christ to solve the sin-virus problem for mankind?

In the final chapters, the multidimensionality of God will be examined, as well as how angels and Jesus Christ are multidimensional beings. Heaven and hell are real places located within the spiritual dimension. Has God communicated with us from where He is to where we are in our three-dimensional world? How do we communicate with God from our three-dimensional world to God's multidimensional location? Finally, how do we live successfully in the three-dimensional world that is connected to the spiritual dimension?

The point of this book is to show how the Bible reveals the spiritual realm as a reality and also to demonstrate how science delivers overwhelming evidence of its existence. Next, the purpose is to demonstrate that if there is a creator, a spiritual realm where He created and resides must exist. Lastly, after establishing the reality of a spiritual realm as a higher dimension, we will have a better or more in-depth understanding of God, angels, Jesus, heaven, hell, time, prayer, worship, and spiritual warfare.

Chapter 1

The Paranormal, the Supernatural, and the Bible

The best data we have are exactly what I would have predicted had I nothing to go on but the five books of Moses, the Psalms, the Bible as a whole, in that the universe appears to have order and purpose.

–Arno Penzias, 1978 Nobel Prize recipient in physics

Anyone who reads the Bible or believes it is God's Word understands the spiritual realm described within its pages. The word *paranormal* is defined by Merriam-Webster as *very strange and not able to be explained by what scientists know about nature and the world.*[9] Angels, demons, and the miraculous events of the Bible are explainable only if we don't discount the spiritual realm or spirit world. The spirit world is often thought of as merely invisible spirits that float around in the three-dimensional world undetected and unseen. Though this concept will be developed in subsequent chapters, what if the spirit world were a higher dimension? We live in three dimensions of space and one dimension of time. What if God, angels, and demons lived in a fourth dimension of space undetectable to people? It would be possible for them to enter the physical dimension, appearing as three-dimensional beings, and then exit into the spiritual realm, once again becoming invisible to the human eye.

The Bible records humanly unexplainable events that are evidence of a fourth dimension or a dimension separate from the three dimensions in which people live. The Bible speaks of a spiritual world that is present within, around, or near the physical world. This world is not directly evident to us, but at various times, the Bible has recorded events that are miraculous or multidimensional. Many people, including scientists, have a difficult time believing in the spiritual realm because it is not something that can be tested or observed in a laboratory. Therefore, people are very resistant to believing in the miraculous events that happened in the Bible, especially in the life of Jesus Christ.

Thomas Jefferson was one of those who did not believe in the miraculous. He liked the moral teachings of Jesus, but saw the miracles recorded in the Gospels as myth or folklore that were added to make Jesus appear greater than He really was. He developed his own story of Jesus from portions of the Gospel books. Owen Edwards, in an article for Smithsonian.com, writes about how Jefferson was dedicated to what Jesus Christ taught His followers, but he did not believe the Gospels were recorded accurately. Edwards claims that Jefferson saw the four Gospel writers as untrustworthy correspondents. "So, Jefferson created his own gospel by taking a sharp instrument, perhaps a penknife, to existing copies of the New Testament and pasting up his own account of Christ's philosophy, distinguishing it from what he called 'the corruption of schismatizing followers.'"[10]

To believe in God, to believe in heaven, to believe that the Bible is the Word of God is to believe in the supernatural. To be a Christian is to believe in a spiritual world that is as real as we can prove the three-dimensional physical world to be. The Bible assumes the reality of the spiritual realm without explaining it or attempting to convince the reader it exists. To read the Bible without believing in the reality of the spiritual realm or while denying the existence of a spiritual realm is to miss the whole point of the teachings and purpose of the writings themselves. That was Thomas Jefferson; he received Jesus' moral teachings, but not the resurrection. Edwards writes, "Much of the material Jefferson elected to not include related to miraculous events, such as the feeding of the multitudes with only two fish and five loaves of barley bread; he eschewed anything that he perceived as 'contrary to reason.' His idiosyncratic gospel concludes with Christ's entombment but omits His resurrection."[11] But the Bible without the spiritual realm is nothing more than a literary book of history with moral teachings or stories to instruct.

What is the spiritual realm? The Bible teaches the reality of a spiritual, invisible and unseen world where angels, both good and evil, reside and do their ministry or work. Heaven and God's throne are located in this realm. Walter C. Kaiser, in *Hard Sayings of the Bible*, writes concerning the spiritual realm in the Bible:

> **The Bible as a whole and the New Testament in particular witness to the existence of nonphysical beings and a spiritual realm. Besides God the Father, there is Jesus, who according to John, once existed completely in this realm and then became flesh (John 1:14). The ascension refers to his return to the spiritual realm, but as a physical being (that is, he remains a human being with a body). Then there are angels, which are referred to 176 times in the New**

Testament, mostly in the Gospels and Revelation. These holy beings point to the existence of a spiritual realm, which, the New Testament says, also contains a dark side.[12]

While the Bible assumes the reality of the spiritual realm, it does not explain it or try to convince the reader it exists. It just reports happenings that are part of the spiritual realm. John writes, "God is spirit"[13] (John 4:24) in the Gospel that bears his name. Additionally, he asserts that, "No one has seen God at any time" (John 1:18). From this, we can know that God is a spiritual being that no one has seen. The Bible, from the very beginning, reveals the spiritual realm to mankind. The Bible records interactions between people and the spiritual dimension as if they are part of normal, everyday life. Angels coming and going, miracles taking place, and heavenly scenes are unveiled in the physical, three-dimensional world. The following events are a few of many in the Word of God that point to a spiritual realm. They are also listed to illustrate where the Bible explicitly points to a spiritual world or realm.

Creation and the Spiritual Realm

"In the beginning God created the heavens and the earth" (Genesis 1:1). The Bible begins from outside the physical realm or outside the three-dimensional universe. In this verse alone, Genesis 1:1, at least three assertions can be identified that point to the existence of the spiritual realm. The first assertion is regarding time. This verse reveals a beginning, a point when time began with a point of initiation or origination. God started the universe's time clock. The apostle Paul in Titus 1:2 writes, "In hope of eternal life which God, who cannot lie, promised before time began." Paul says here that God made a promise before time began. The Greek word translated *time* in this verse (translated *world* in the KJV) is *aiōnios*. This word is found seventy-one times in the New Testament. It is translated *eternal, everlasting, and forever*, sixty-eight of those times.[14] The remaining three times the word is used, it is paired up with the Greek word *chronos*, and they are translated together as *since the world began* (Romans 16:25) and *before time began* (2 Timothy 1:9; Titus 1:2). The Greek word *chronos* indicates time.[15] The English words *chronology* and *chronological* come from this root. God's promise was made before time began. Hugh Ross, in his book, *Beyond the Cosmos*, writes:

> **Paul states here that our time dimension had a beginning and implies that God created our time dimension. These verses tell us that God engaged in cause and effect behavior before our time dimension existed. Thus, there must be at least the equivalent of a second dimension of time for God.[16]**

If God created the universe and the arrow of time that flows from the beginning of time towards the end, then He is outside of our dimension of time. Time is connected with our three dimensions of space in this world. The fact that God is outside the dimension of time places Him outside of the connected three dimensions of space also.

The second assertion from Genesis 1:1 is that God created space. He created the physical, three-dimensional world. Therefore, God must be outside of the three (or more) dimensions that He created. Thanks to Albert Einstein, the world understands that the relationship between space and time has a much deeper meaning. Space and time impact each other; the changing of one must change the other. Ken Ham, founder and president of Answers in Genesis, writing about Genesis 1:1, states:

> **A study of this verse reveals that God created time, space, and matter on the first day of Creation Week. No one of these can have a meaningful existence without the others. God created the space-mass-time universe. Space and matter must exist in time, and time requires space and matter. Time is only meaningful if physical entities exist and events transpire during time.**[17]

God is greater than, and outside of, the space and time He created.

The third assertion taken from Genesis 1:1 is that God created the spiritual realm itself. He created angels and the dimensional space in which they reside. This verse states that God created the heavens. Included in that word *heavens* is the spiritual realm. Most scholars believe the heavens include three regions. The first region is the earth's atmosphere—the air and clouds, where birds fly and planes soar. The second region is the universe, where the earth resides. This includes planets, suns, moons, stars, galaxies, and all thirteen billion light-years of the physical universe. The third region included in the word *heavens* is the spiritual realm—the unseen world where angels, good and evil are found. Though we'll elaborate further later, it is very possible that included in the word *heavens* are the various dimensional realms which would include Paradise. Therefore, God must be outside of or greater than the three dimensions of space and one dimension of time known as the physical realm. He is also greater than the spiritual realm in which angels live. Paul, in Colossians 1:16, says that God created the spiritual realm and all that is entailed in it. “For by Him all things were created that are in heaven and that are on earth, visible and invisible, whether thrones or dominions or principalities or powers. All things were created through Him and for Him.” Paul states that it is through Jesus Christ that all things were created. Paul claims that all things were created by God through Jesus Christ, visible and invisible. That means all things and beings in the three-dimensional world and all things and beings in the spiritual realm. Nehemiah 9:6 states that God created heaven and the hosts that dwell within the heavens. “You alone are the LORD; You have made heaven, the heaven of heavens, with all their host, the earth and everything on it, the seas and all that is in them, and You preserve them all. The host of heaven worships You.” God created even Satan; he was created good, but he sinned and fell from his perfect, created position and state. Ezekiel 28:15 says, “You were perfect in your ways from the day you were created, till iniquity was found in you.”

The Angels that Visit Abraham and the Spiritual Realm

Angels are the greatest example of beings that live in the spiritual realm. Angels entering into man's three-dimensional world demonstrate that there is a spiritual dimension from which the angels come. The first mention of the word *angel* in the Bible takes place in Genesis 16. The passage is talking about the Angel of the Lord. The next passage speaking of angels is Genesis 19. This is where two of the three angels that had visited Abraham and Sarah were on their way to Sodom and Gomorrah. "Then the LORD appeared to him by the terebinth trees of Mamre, as he was sitting in the tent door in the heat of the day. So he lifted his eyes and looked, and behold, three men were standing by him; and when he saw them, he ran from the tent door to meet them, and bowed himself to the ground" (Genesis 18:1-2). "Now the two angels came to Sodom in the evening, and Lot was sitting in the gate of Sodom. When Lot saw them, he rose to meet them, and he bowed himself with his face toward the ground" (Genesis 19:1).

This is the beginning of many angelic events that are recorded throughout the Bible. Angels are spiritual beings, but they appear to be three-dimensional beings at times. From Genesis to Revelation, angels are all over the pages of the Word of God. Even in present-day society, many believe in angels, though much of what is believed is from movies and books rather than Scripture.

In Genesis 18, three men visit Abraham and eat with him. It is later discovered in chapter 19 that two of these men are angels, and the third is the Angel of the Lord. The *Holman Old Testament Commentary* makes this indication:

> **Suddenly he saw three men standing nearby. These were no ordinary visitors, since the chapter begins with the words *the Lord appeared to Abraham,* and two of them are called angels in 19:1. Many scholars identify the third person of this group as the Lord himself (another Christophany).**[18]

An interesting thing occurs with these spiritual beings. They appear human to Abraham and the readers of the story. If it were not for the next chapter, if we had only chapter 18, then one would believe these were mere men (two of them at the very least). One of the reasons is that these three angels ate food with Abraham like a human would. "And Abraham ran to the herd, took a tender and good calf, gave it to a young man, and he hastened to prepare it. So he took butter and milk and the calf which he had prepared, and set it before them; and he stood by them under the tree as they ate" (Genesis 18:7-8).

Genesis 19 identifies two of these men as angels as they go to Sodom. When they enter the city, they meet with Lot, Abraham's nephew. It is not stated whether Lot recognizes the men as angels, but he does know them as new to the city. When the angels express to Lot that they will spend the night in the streets of the city, Lot protests and urges them to stay with him, and they comply. While in Lot's home, the angels once again eat food. The men of the city begin banging on Lot's front door, demanding that his new guests be put outside so they can have sexual relations with them. This disturbing event not only exposes the deplorable character of the people of Sodom, but it also shows that they thought these angels were men, just like themselves. Lot pleads with the men of Sodom to depart and leave his house, but they will not listen. They become violent with Lot, so the angels grab Lot and bring him in the house. The angels then strike the men outside with blindness. This is a supernatural power that God allows the angels to use. Genesis 19:10-11 relates, "But the men reached out their hands and pulled Lot into the house with them, and shut the door. And they struck the men who were at the doorway of the house with blindness, both small and great, so that they became weary trying to find the door." These angelic spiritual beings that appear to be human have miraculous powers. The angels also display human characteristics when they urge Lot and his family to leave the city by grabbing their hands and leading them out.

We see an overlapping of the spiritual and physical realms when it comes to angels coming and going. At times angels are invisible and unseen; other times, they are in human form and look like any other human being of their day.

Moses and the Spiritual Realm

Moses experienced many events that can be explained only by the spiritual realm. Moses' life is one of many miracles and spiritual-dimension events. His miraculous encounters begin with a burning bush that is not burned up, from which he hears the voice of God. Hugh Ross says,

> **In many biblical passages God manifests himself in our dimensions in ways that seem strange to human**

> **observers. He speaks to Moses from a burning bush that does not burn up. The Israelites see him in a pillar of cloud by day and of fire by night. His voice hits their ears like thunderclaps. God's "finger" inscribes the Ten Commandments in stone.**[19]

The life of Moses is divided into three forty-year segments. Moses lived forty years in Egypt, forty years as a shepherd in the land of Midian, and forty years wandering in the wilderness of Sinai after he led the Israelites out of Egypt. It was during Moses' last forty years when nearly all of God's multidimensional, miraculous works took place in his life. God used Moses to bring ten plagues upon Egypt and primarily upon Pharaoh. God led the Israelites out of Egypt and through the parting of the Red Sea. God spoke to Moses several times. God provided water for millions of Israelites from a rock. God provided manna for the Israelites to gather every day except the Sabbath. The many unusual and miraculous events during the life and ministry of Moses make the spiritual realm or dimension a very credible reality.

Jesus and the Spiritual Realm

The life, death and resurrection of Jesus Christ is the pinnacle of the spiritual dimension crossing over into the physical world. The life of Jesus begins with the spiritual realm by angels appearing to Mary and Joseph. Jesus' birth is a combination of the spiritual realm and the physical world. Jesus is God in the flesh. He was born of a virgin, who was impregnated by the Holy Spirit. Jesus' ministry is full of the miraculous and unexplainable in the physical realm. The blind received sight, the lame walked, the deaf received their hearing, the dead were raised, and those with sicknesses were healed. The demon possessed were set free and, most of all, people's sins were forgiven. Jesus walked on water, stilled a storm, fed thousands of people with a few fish and five loaves of bread, turned water into wine, and appeared transfigured into a glorified state on a mountain, along with Moses and Elijah.

The most incredible event is the death, burial, and resurrection of Jesus Christ. Christ rose from the dead and was then seen by over five hundred people. Jesus had an earthly body during His ministry. When He was resurrected from the dead, His body was different but still had similarities with His earthly body. He told Thomas to touch His hands and side; He was physical. He ate food, cooked, walked, and talked. But he appeared in a closed room out of nowhere and then vanished from the room. He walked with two men on the road to Emmaus and then vanished from their sight. In his book, *The World of the Unseen*, Arthur Willink writes concerning Jesus' resurrected body:

> **His Body, having entered and returned from the grave, was freed from all its imperfections, freed from the bonds which had confined it to our Space. Thus, there is no difficulty in perceiving how it was that at Emmaus He vanished out of the sight of the two Disciples. He simply passed along the unseen path into the Higher Space, where their eyes could not follow Him.**[20]

The resurrected body of Jesus Christ was physical, yet spiritual and eternal. He appeared as flesh and bone, not as a spirit, and He had access to the spiritual realm or world. Was Jesus' resurrected body fashioned in such a way that He could live in both the three-dimensional world and in the spiritual dimension of heaven?

Paul and the Spiritual Realm

The Apostle Paul, writing to the church in Ephesus, states:

> **Finally, my brethren, be strong in the Lord and in the power of His might. Put on the whole armor of God, that you may be able to stand against the wiles of the devil. For we do not wrestle against flesh and blood, but against principalities, against powers, against the rulers of the darkness of this age, against spiritual hosts of wickedness in the heavenly places. Therefore take up the whole armor of God, that you may be able to withstand in the evil day, and having done all, to stand (Ephesians 6:10-13).**

Paul clearly identifies the spiritual realm as a reality to the follower of Christ. The Christian can expect to be attacked from this spiritual world, so Paul gives instructions for protecting oneself and for waging combat against beings in the spiritual realm.

> **For though we walk in the flesh, we do not war according to the flesh. For the weapons of our warfare are not carnal but mighty in God for pulling down strongholds, casting down arguments and every high thing that exalts itself against the knowledge of God, bringing every thought into captivity to the obedience of Christ (2 Corinthians 10:3-5).**

A Person's Spirit

The Bible distinctly teaches that people are more than physical beings; they are also spiritual. There is more to a person than the physical body, brain function, and muscle memory. The following is a sampling of the many verses in the Bible that point to a person's spiritual nature in addition to the physical nature:

> **Then the dust will return to the earth as it was, and the spirit will return to God who gave it (Ecclesiastes 12:7).**

> **For as the body without the spirit is dead, so faith without works is dead also (James 2:26).**

> **Now may the God of peace Himself sanctify you completely; and may your whole spirit, soul, and body be preserved blameless at the coming of our Lord Jesus Christ (1 Thessalonians 5:23).**

> **For what profit is it to a man if he gains the whole world, and loses his own soul? Or what will a man give in exchange for his soul? (Matthew 16:26)**

> **So we are always confident, knowing that while we are at home in the body we are absent from the Lord. For we walk by faith, not by sight. We are confident, yes, well pleased rather to be absent from the body and to be present with the Lord (2 Corinthians 5:6-8).**

> **For God so loved the world that He gave His only begotten Son, that whoever believes in Him should not perish but have everlasting life (John 3:16).**

> **Jesus said to her, "I am the resurrection and the life. He who believes in Me, though he may die, he shall live. And whoever lives and believes in Me shall never die. Do you believe this?" (John 11:25-26)**

These verses teach that a person is eternal and will live forever. If the body dies, then something immaterial must live on—the person's spirit. A body has mass; it is made up of atoms and molecules. The spirit has no mass; it is immaterial and spiritual. The consciousness or spirit is the functioning part of a person's body. The body is what allows the spirit to live in this three-dimensional world and interpret the available data using the five senses, intellect, and reasoning. Chuck Missler in his book, *Beyond Time & Space*, writes:

> **We have an additional dimensionality—whether we call it soul or spirit—that is not subject to the laws of physics or the betrayals of time, because it has no mass. Our outward man is in a temporary environment, subject to the destructive forces of thermal decay, but our inward man is beyond the leash of time and is therefore eternal. The Apostle Paul never claimed to be a physicist, of course, but he understood these things better than most of us, sharing their mysteries with the Corinthians when he said:**
>
> ***For which cause we faint not; but though our outward man perish, yet the inward man is renewed day by day. For our light affliction, which is but for a moment, worketh for us a far more exceeding and eternal weight of glory; While we look not at the things which are seen, but at the things which are not seen: for the things which are seen are temporal; but the things which are not seen are eternal* (2 Corinthians 4:16-18).**[21]

While these examples alone are sufficient to establish the reality of the spiritual realm, the Bible contains many more examples of the spiritual realm intersecting with the physical realm.

Chapter 2

Step into the Next Dimension

Geometry is unique and eternal, a reflection of the mind of God. That men are able to participate in it is one of the reasons why man is an image of God.

–*Johannes Kepler (1571 - 1630)*

God is like a skillful Geometrician.

–*Sir Thomas Browne, Religio Medici*

He [Bernard Riemann] was far ahead of his time. Sixty years later, Einstein was able to finally apply Riemann's mathematics when dealing with the curvature of space-time. Riemann was the first to lay the mathematical foundation of geometry in higher dimensional space—what we call hyperspace.

–Chuck *Missler, Beyond Perception: The Evidence of Things Not Seen*

"Angels are real. They are spiritual beings that primarily dwell in the spiritual dimension, a higher dimension than the three dimensions in which we live." This is what I would say to the class I was teaching on the topic of angels. "What does it mean to dwell in a higher dimension," I would ask the class. "The best way to understand what a four-dimensional being might be like in three dimensions is to understand what a three-dimensional being or object would be like in two dimensions." I would then take out a piece of blank white paper and draw a stick figure of a man on the paper that I would call "Flatman." "Flatman," I would explain, "lives in the two-dimensional world much like this piece of paper. The two-dimensional plane in which he lives goes on forever in each direction. The only thing Flatman knows is the two-dimensional world in which he lives. If a three-dimensional object were to pass through his two-dimensional plane, he would see only what intersected with his world. If a three-dimensional finger were to pass through Flatman's plane, he would see only a circle or the shape that intersected his two-dimensional world. "Take any object," I would say, "and as it passes through Flatman's plane, he would see and know only what intersects with his two-dimensional plane. A three-dimensional object can be right next to Flatman's world, and he has no idea it exists until it touches his two-dimensional plane. Whatever three-dimensional object passes through Flatman's world becomes two-dimensional to Flatman. He sees objects only in two dimensions."

I would then relate this concept to us seeing and experiencing a four-dimensional object or being when it enters our three-dimensional world. "When an angel," I explained, "comes into our three-dimensional world, he appears three-dimensional to us. As an angel enters into our three-dimensional realm, he looks like any other three-dimensional being. The angel could be right next to our three-dimensional world, just like an object could be right next to Flatman's two-dimensional world, and we would not know it even exists. When God gives the angel permission or a command to do so, he moves one millimeter into our three-dimensional world and appears as a three-dimensional man." I would then elaborate, "Maybe this is where heaven is, right next to us in the next dimension. When we die, perhaps we move one millimeter into the next dimension, where we enter heaven." This would always awaken an interest in the spiritual dimension of where heaven is, where angels are, and where God is at the present time. Understanding the spiritual realm as a higher dimension with spatial dimensionality and locality is a very important part of the Bible and our Christian beliefs, but it is difficult to comprehend. This chapter begins at the foundation of spatial dimensions by looking at what they are. After establishing spatial dimensions, we will then attempt to understand higher dimensions or hyperdimensions.

First, what are dimensions? A spatial dimension is an extent in a direction. In a three-dimensional world, that would be the length, then height, then width. These are directional, in that each space is perpendicular to the other. Therefore, a dimension is a measure of extent. "The most common connotation is spatial extent, as in the dimensions of a rectangular block—i.e. its length, width, and depth,"[22] writes Chris McMullen. He then differentiates between dimensions and dimensionality. "The dimensionality of a space or an object refers to the number of independent directions into which it extends."[23] McMullen then lists several examples of objects with different dimensionality:

- **A single point, infinitesimal in size, has no spatial extent. Points are zero-dimensional because they extend in zero directions.**

- **A line segment, extending along a single direction, is one-dimensional (1D, for short).**
- **A rectangle is 2D, as it extends along two independent directions—length and width.**
- **A 3D rectangular block has a third independent direction—depth.[24]**

We live in three dimensions of space: length, height, and width. This is the space we move around in. Three dimensions have volume. Cubes, pyramids, cones, and spheres are examples of three-dimensional objects. Objects in this world have volume; they are three-dimensional. Houses, cars, trees, lakes, and boats are examples of three-dimensional objects in this world, and this list could go on and on. Zero-dimensional space has no freedom of movement. One-dimensional space can only move back and forth on a line with one direction of freedom of movement. Two-dimensional space is movement in a plane. It has two directions of freedom of movement. Three-dimensional space has three directions of movement. William Granville in his book, *The Fourth Dimension and the Bible,* states:

> **A point in our space has three degrees of freedom. It can move to the right or left, forward or backward, and up or down. For instance, an article in a rectangular-shaped room may be moved from one place to any other by moving it parallel to the directions of the length, breadth, and height of the room. The reader can reach no place which may not be reached by going north or south, east or west, and upward or downward.[25]**

Rudolf Rucker, in his book, *Geometry, Relativity and the Fourth Dimension,* writes about the three-dimensional world in which we live:

> **We live in three-dimensional space. That is, motion in our space has three degrees of freedom—no fewer and no more. In other words, we have mutually perpendicular types of motion (left/right, forward/backward, up/down), and any point in our space can be reached by combining the three possible types of motion (e.g., "Walk straight ahead about 200 paces to the river, then go right about 50 paces until you come to a big oak tree. Climb about 40 feet up into it. I'll be waiting for you there.") Normally it is difficult for us to perform up/down motions; space is more three-dimensional for a bird or a fish than it is for us. On the other hand, space is essentially one-dimensional for a car driving down a two-lane road, essentially two-dimensional for a snowmobile or a car driving around an empty parking lot.[26]**

We experience three-dimensional space daily. What would a higher dimension be like? How would we experience a fourth dimension of space? Concerning higher dimensions, sometimes referred to as hyperdimensions, Chuck Missler writes:

> **The word hyperdimension comes from the Greek word ὑπέρ—hyper—which means "over" or "above" or "beyond." Hyperdimension is really just a fancy word for more than three spatial dimensions. You and I are used to three spatial dimensions—length, width and height—but when we deal with the additional dimensions beyond those we can see with our physical eyes, we're dealing in hyperdimensions. We're moving past plane geometry and even three-dimensional Euclidean geometry.[27]**

Higher dimensions are really understood only mathematically. The truth is seen in an equation or in logical geometry that possibly points to the reality. Picturing a higher dimension is beyond difficult. It is so different from our three-dimensional thinking that it poses a great challenge.

In order to begin contemplating a fourth dimension or a higher dimension, it is always best to begin with the lower dimensions. Take a lower dimension and stretch it to a dimension higher. If a zero-dimensional space (a point) moves in any direction, any distance, there would be a line. That is, if a zero-dimensional point is moved one unit to the right, there is now a one-dimensional line. If a one-dimensional line of one inch moved perpendicular to itself, any distance, one would have a plane. It would be a square plane if it moved one inch. If a two-dimensional square moved perpendicular to itself the same distance as one of its sides, it would be a cube. Now that is as far as we can go in the world of three dimensions. But if this process continued and if the cube could move perpendicular to itself, it would create a four-dimensional space. This is called a tesseract. Granville writes:

> **We cannot conceive of a motion perpendicular to a cube (*i.e.*, a single motion perpendicular to all the faces of the cube, or, as it may also be stated, perpendicular to any three adjacent edges of the cube). Not one of our senses calls for a fourth direction perpendicular to the other three, experience leaves us satisfied with three dimensions. We cannot visualize the tesseract but it is possible for us to construct a figure in our space which will symbolize the tesseract, that is, a figure having many of the properties of the tesseract.**[28]

A cube would have six sides, and a tesseract or hypercube would have twenty-four sides. Figure 2.1. illustrates the movements to a higher dimension.

Figure 2.1. Movement to a higher dimension

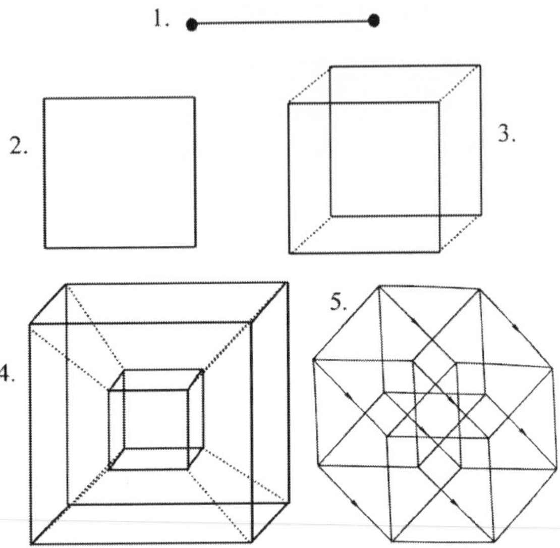

1. Zero-dimensional to One-dimensional
2. One-dimensional to Two-dimensional
3. Two-dimensional to Three-dimensional
4. Three-dimensional cube to Four-dimensional Tesseract
5. Three-dimensional cube to Four-dimensional Hypercube

Note: Object 5., the four-dimensional hypercube, is taken from Rudy v. B. Rucker, Geometry, Relativity, and the Fourth Dimension (New York: Dover Publications, 1977), 2.

A good way to explain the next higher dimension is to explain going from two dimensions to three dimensions as I did to begin this chapter. The concept is normally attributed to Edwin A. Abbott who wrote a nineteenth-century satire called, *Flatland: A Romance of Many Dimensions.* In his novel he writes about a world that is flat, Flatland. In Flatland all the inhabitants live in a two-dimensional plane. The Flatland narrator's name is A Square.[29] A Square meets a character, A Sphere, from a three-dimensional world called Spaceland. As A Sphere crosses through Flatland, the Flatlanders see only what intersects with their world. As A Sphere begins to touch Flatland, a dot is seen. Then, as A Sphere continues to move through Flatland, they see a small circle that enlarges slowly to the full width of A Sphere's diameter. The circle grows smaller and smaller as A Sphere exits Flatland.[30] A Square tries to explain to his fellow Flatlanders that A Sphere is really a higher dimensional object, but the message is not received well.[31] A Square meets much resistance from the Flatlanders to this new and crazy idea of a higher dimension. A Square is finally arrested and placed in jail.[32] The book helps a person see the differences between a two-dimensional world and a three-dimensional world. Many similar differences might exist between a three-dimensional world and a four-dimensional world.

Using the message of the book *Flatland* as a mental springboard, many people have made similar analogies to help picture what a four-dimensional object would look like in a three-dimensional world. Picture in your mind a man that lives in a plane of glass. His name is Flatman. The plane of glass extends forever in all directions of its two dimensions. A three-dimensional object can touch the glass, but Flatman sees only what touches the glass or plane he lives in. If a basketball touched the plane, Flatman would see a small circle that touches his dimension. If a hand was pressed up against Flatman's world, he would see the outline of a hand. Taking the analogy one step farther, Flatman's plane can be passed through. If the basketball began to penetrate Flatman's plane, he would see only what intersected with his world. It would be a two-dimensional circle. If we inserted a pencil into Flatman's world, he would see a small circle (the tip of the pencil) and the circle would get larger the farther it was inserted. Then the pencil passes completely through the plane until it vanishes. Flatman can see only what intersects with his dimension. The pencil or basketball can be one millimeter from his world or plane, and yet he has no idea it exists based on what he can see. A whole world of three-dimensional objects can be close to his world without him having any idea where they are or that they even exist.

Using this analogy from a two-dimensional world to a three-dimensional world, think of how that would correlate from a three-dimensional world to a four-dimensional world. If a four-dimensional object were to enter a three-dimensional world, only what intersects with the three dimensions would be seen. For example, if an angel is four-dimensional, but he enters the three-dimensional world, he appears three-dimensional. A resurrected Jesus Christ entering the three-dimensional world would appear as a three-dimensional Jesus Christ.

What about location? Perhaps angels are not merely invisible creatures flying around in the physical world.

Maybe angels are right next to the three-dimensional world, and they can enter in when God permits or commands. When they enter the three-dimensional world, they appear as men. Where is heaven located? Maybe heaven is in a higher dimension. The basketball was right next to Flatman's world, but he did not know it existed until it touched or intersected with his two-dimensional world. Heaven could be right next to the three-dimensional world without our being able to detect it. Heaven could be one millimeter from our three-dimensional world right now. When a person dies, he would move one millimeter into the next dimension, heaven. It's possible that a world of four-dimensional objects exists right next to our three-dimensional world. These objects would include angels, demons, heaven, hell, Jesus Christ, heavenly believers, and God's throne.

Returning to Flatman's world of two dimensions, suppose a man wearing boots is walking on Flatman's two-dimensional world. Flatman would see only the outline or prints of this man's boots. Flatman would see four independent objects: a print from the heel and a print from the toe of one boot, and a duplicate set of prints from the second boot (see Figure 2.2.). The shapes seem strange to Flatman as he wonders what they are or what they mean.

Figure 2.2. Two-dimensional footprints

What conclusions can Flatman draw from the boot prints? Are they connected? Are there four different beings or objects? What do these objects represent? It is impossible, without more specific revelation, for Flatman to know that one man wearing boots has made these two-dimensional prints. Could this be how it is for three-dimensional people to understand a higher dimensional God? The information is broken down so basic for us to understand, that it only gives a footprint of who God really is to our three-dimensional minds. Is this what Paul talked about when he said in 1 Corinthians 13:12, "For now we see in a mirror, dimly, but then face to face. Now I know in part, but then I shall know just as I also am known"? Just because the next dimension is not easily detectable to us, it does not necessarily mean that there is no higher dimension. The Bible delivers clues to us that point to a higher dimension.

Is understanding higher dimensions like explaining objects to a blind person who has been blind since birth? Is trying to comprehend spiritual dimensions like a blind person trying to comprehend colors? How would one go about explaining the moon, stars, sun, or even our solar system to the blind? They cannot touch them. They must take a person's word that what they are hearing is true. The sun may be the easiest because blind people can feel its warmth on their skin. An experience through the physical senses can corroborate the explanation being given. Is this like a person trying to understand the spiritual dimension and receiving a three-dimensional confirmation about a spiritual truth? One example might be experiencing the spiritual truth of forgiveness in this three-dimensional world by receiving forgiveness from someone for a wrong done to them. This experience of feeling forgiven, or being extended forgiveness that is not deserved, can open one's eyes to the forgiveness offered by the multidimensional God spoken of in the Bible.

Chapter 3

Time Machines and Twilight Zones

I find it as difficult to understand a scientist who does not acknowledge the presence of a superior rationality behind the existence of the universe as it is to comprehend a theologian who would deny the advances of science. And there is certainly no scientific reason why God cannot retain the same relevance in our modern world that He held before we began probing His creation with a telescope, cyclotron, and space vehicles. Can a physicist visualize an electron? The electron is materially inconceivable, and yet it is so perfectly known through its effects that we use it to illuminate our cities, guide our airlines through the night skies, and take the most accurate measurements. What strange rationale makes some physicists accept the inconceivable electron as real while refusing to accept the reality of God on the ground that they cannot conceive him? My relationship with God is very personal. I think you can be on first name terms with Him, you know, and tell Him what your troubles are, and ask for help. I do it all the time, and it works for me.

–Werhner von Braun, NASA engineer and scientist, designer of the Saturn rockets

Science and Albert Einstein opened the door to time-travel stories and *Twilight Zone* episodes. Science fiction took off in the early 1900s. Scientists were discovering just how supernatural the universe really was. The lines began to blur between science and fiction. The purpose of this chapter is to lay a foundation for higher dimensions from a scientific perspective. Before the nineteenth century, theories about higher dimensions were mostly philosophical and not scientific. Once Einstein shared the theory of relativity with the rest of the world, new scientific doors were opened in considering higher dimensions. It is worth the time required to briefly summarize the significant events in the scientific path that led to Einstein's theory and eventually to quantum theory and string theory.

Galileo and Newton: The Beginning of Modern Science

Science and physics seek to discover the why and how concerning motion and the forces in the universe. Galileo made many discoveries and advances in science. Galileo created what is known today as the modern scientific method. He would come up with a theory or postulation, then do experiments to try to prove or disprove the theory. Based on the outcome of the experiments, Galileo would draw his conclusions. The tests he performed about motion and relativity played a massive role in advancing scientific knowledge. Galileo used the example of a man on top of a ship's mast (ships were an excellent example of a moving vehicle in his time) holding a ball (such as a small cannonball). If the man were to drop the cannonball and let it fall toward the ship's deck, what would happen? If the ship were moving, the cannonball would drop straight down. And if the ship were stationary, the cannonball would still fall straight down. If one were to throw the cannonball straight up while the ship was moving, the cannonball would come straight back down. However, to a person on shore watching the man drop the cannonball from the ship's mast, the action would look a bit different. If the ship were moving, the cannonball would not only be falling straight down toward the ship's deck, but it would also be moving as the ship moves forward—as in Figure 3.1.[33]

Figure 3.1. Falling ball perspective to one on the ship versus one on the shore

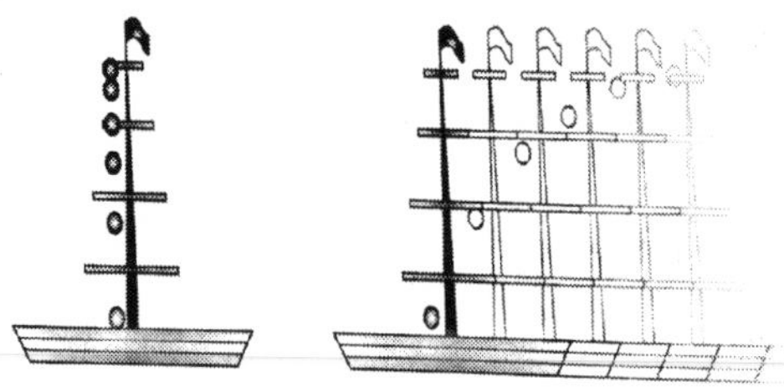

Source: Figure 8-1 from Carlos I. Calle, *Einstein for Dummies* (Hoboken, NJ: Wiley Publishing, 2005), 114.

Galileo's conclusions about the experiment of dropping a cannonball from the mast of the ship helped him to argue the theory that the earth was moving. Opponents of the moving earth would say that if the earth were moving and one threw a ball in the air, then it would not come straight back down. Galileo proved that if the earth were moving, the man was moving, and the ball was moving, then the ball would come straight back down. Galileo established the principle of relativity. "According to Galileo, you can't distinguish steady motion in a straight line from rest. If you can't distinguish the two, they are the same. Uniform motion (as Galileo called it) and rest are the same thing."[34]

Sir Isaac Newton took Galileo's laws and expanded them to apply to the universe. Newton is best remembered for an apple that fell from a tree, leading to the theory of gravity. Newton sought to answer the question of why the earth revolves around the sun and why the earth pulls toward the sun. What keeps the moon in space, without falling to earth? Is dropping a cannonball from a mast of a ship the same force that keeps the earth in its orbit around the sun and the moon in its orbit around the earth? Of all Newton's work, the universal law of gravitation, as we now call it, is considered his greatest discovery.[35] But he had to invent new mathematics to accomplish the discovery—it is known as calculus.

Newton developed a theory of gravity that was based upon mass, especially very large mass. "In Newton's gravitational theory, the force between two objects is based on the product of their masses, divided by the square of the distance between them. In other words, the heavier the two objects are, the more force there is between them, assuming the distance between them stays the same."[36] Gravity force, or power, increases as two large objects, like the sun and a planet, get closer together. Gravity has an inverse square relationship. This means that the closer the objects get to each other, the force increases. If the distance is reduced by fifty percent between the two objects, the force increases by four times. The opposite is also true. If the distance is doubled, the force decreases by four times, to twenty-five percent.[37] Through observation and mathematical equations, Newton was able to demonstrate his theory of how gravity worked. Nevertheless, Newton never figured out why gravity does what it does.

Galileo's work on motion laid the foundation for Newton's discoveries. Newton's discoveries and astronomical studies of the universe and the motion of planets paved the way for Einstein's theories. As a result of Newton's work, the universe appeared to be very predictable and mathematical. Everything worked like a precise clock. Time was not relative, and it was the same everywhere for everyone. "Einstein's universe is very different. The theory of relativity tells us that time and space aren't fixed. They change depending on how the observer moves."[38]

Einstein's Relativity Revolution

In 1905 Albert Einstein introduced the theory of special relativity to the world. It was based on two critical principles:

> ***The principle of relativity: The laws of physics don't change, even for objects moving in inertial (constant speed) frames of reference.***
>
> ***The principle of the speed of light: The speed of light is the same for all observers, regardless of their motion relative to the light source. (Physicists write this speed using the symbol c.)***[39]

One of the exciting findings from Einstein's special theory of relativity was that the speed of light was constant, and time was not constant. Many believed that time would obviously be constant. Most scientists and people questioned how time could change. Instead of proving that time could change, scientists set out to see if the speed of light was constant. Every time an experiment was done, the speed of light never changed. If the speed of light did not change, then time could change, according to Einstein.

Einstein added an exciting philosophical angle to science by showing that space and time are intertwined.

> **According to relativity, the combination of your motion through time and your motion through space equals exactly the speed of light. This combination of the three dimensions of space and the one of time became what was later called *spacetime*, a four-dimensional entity that shows that space and time are not separate like Newton thought, but intermixed.**[40]

Science and science fiction also began to merge as the talk of dimensions, time travel, and the warping of spacetime increased around the world.

Newton discovered what gravity was; now Einstein was explaining how gravity worked, and it was mind-blowing. Einstein proposed that space was being warped by the giant mass of the planets and sun. Imagine a trampoline in someone's yard. In the middle of the trampoline lay a bowling ball. The bowling ball would sink into the center, causing a depression that would warp the fabric of the trampoline. If a smaller ball were thrown onto the trampoline, it would roll towards the bowling ball because of the deeper depression in the middle. Einstein proposed that the sun was much like the bowling ball on the trampoline. The sun, with its huge mass, sinks into the fabric of space and a smaller planet will be drawn towards the sun because of the depression that it is making in the fabric of space.

> **Einstein's theory of general relativity has been around for nearly a century and has met every challenge—at least when applied to objects larger than a molecule. [At the quantum level] general relativity begins to break down. The equations make no sense, and space-time becomes an exotic, tumultuous mess of energy fluctuations...String theory (hopefully) represents one way of reconciling gravity at this realm.**[41]

A scientist named Theodore Kaluza was attempting to develop a theory that would unify the forces of gravity and electromagnetism. Kaluza sent a letter describing his equations to Einstein in 1919. "Kaluza took the gravitational field equations of general relativity and wrote them in five dimensions, obtaining results that included Maxwell's equations of electromagnetism!"[42] Though Kaluza did not unify the two forces entirely with mathematics, he did get scientists to look at adding dimensions to equations to see if the math worked. In 1926 Oskar Klein went over Kaluza's work and suggested that a fourth spatial dimension could be rolled up very small, in a little, bitty circular form. The Kaluza-Klein theory never took off then, but it was revisited in the 1970s when string theory was introduced. "As physicists began to realize that string theory contained extra dimensions, the original Kaluza-Klein theory served as an example from the past. Physicists once again curled up the extra dimensions, as Klein had done, so they were essentially undetectable."[43] With the use of extra dimensions mathematically to unify the forces, science had taken an exciting and perhaps "spiritual" direction.

Opening the Door to the Mystical

With science on the front page in many newspapers in the early 1900s, extra dimensions became an interesting fascination to many people. Although this author believes that these dimensions point towards the spiritual dimension in the Bible, others used this dimensional enthusiasm to open a mystical and psychic door. Some truly believed in the dimensions as doorways to the spiritual world. Others used the mystical talk to deceive people and mislead them into thinking they were talking to dead relatives. The media of the day helped feed into the hysteria and hype surrounding dimensions and time distortion or time travel. Space travel stories began to gain overnight interest as people opened their minds to far-out possibilities. The world of science had changed so much in just a few years; who knew what another fifty years would bring? Stories and imaginations ran wild with space creatures, aliens, and far away galaxies.

It was Bernard Riemann's four-dimensional geometry in the late 1800s that possibly sparked the fire that led to the psychics and mystics declaring the door to the afterlife and the dead was now open.

> **A strange cast of characters seized upon Riemann's ideas soon after his famous lecture. American psychic Henry Slade achieved notoriety in 1877 when Leipzig physics professor Johann Zöllner rushed to the former's defense of magic parlor tricks and ghosts by claiming that what was impossible in our ordinary three-dimensional world was readily possible if a**

> **fourth dimension were added. Unfortunately, the ensuing uproar led more to popular turn-of-the-century science fiction, and an impetus for ESP and psychic research...[44]**

H.G. Wells' masterpiece, *The Time Machine,* came out before Einstein's theory of relativity was published. Paul Halpern holds a Ph.D. in physics and has authored several books. He writes,

> **It is a commonplace belief that Einsteinian relativity, developed in the early twentieth century, ushered in the concept of a four-dimensional cosmos. In truth, the idea of time as the fourth dimension dates back much further than that. The fact that H. G. Wells in his 1895 novella *The Time Machine* wrote that "there are really four dimensions, three which we call the three planes of Space, and a fourth, Time," suggests earlier interest in the subject.[45]**

Perhaps the attraction to the higher dimensions and time travel took off with H. G. Wells. But it was accelerated by science, especially the idea that time was elastic and space was like fabric—they were able to stretch. Newspapers want to sell papers, so putting headlines on the front page that get people's attention is paramount.

> **On 28 September 1911 the *Ellensburg Capital,* a newspaper based in the state of Washington, published a front-page article headlined "The Fourth Dimension" claiming that intoxication stimulated the pineal gland and enabled drunkards to see four-dimensional shapes. As the article states: "The shapes which the layman believes the patient only imagines are really seen and are rendered visible through the excitation of the pineal gland, which now is the rudimentary organ of what once was psychic vision."[46]**

Many of the self-proclaimed psychics and mystics capitalized on the hype and began to work in the beginning of the twentieth century. Famous illusionist Harry Houdini is well renowned for his debunking of several psychic frauds. It is believed that he attempted to contact his dead mother using mediums. After supposedly "hearing from his dead mother" during a séance, Houdini realized it was a hoax. Barry Bradford writes:

> **[Sir Arthur] Doyle's wife held a seance at which Houdini's mother "guided" Lady Doyle's hand to write a message to her grieving son. "Oh my darling, thank God, thank God, at last I'm through. I've tried, oh so often—now I am happy. Why, of course, I want to talk to my boy—my own beloved boy—friends, thank you, with all my heart for this." After the séance, Houdini wrote a note on the bottom of the paper: "Message written by Lady Doyle claiming the spirit of my dear Mother had control of her hand—my sainted mother could not write English and spoke broken English."**[47]

He found all psychics and mediums to be frauds, merely using tricks as he would do to entertain audiences. The difference was that the psychics were claiming to really be communicating with the dead. Houdini purposed much of his life to uncovering the tricks that the psychics used to mislead people.

Once the possibility for a fifth dimension was introduced by the Kaluza-Klein theory, science fiction was taking off at the speed of light. *The Twilight Zone* was one of the sci-fi shows that enthralled audiences.

> **As scientists moved on to the fifth dimension, so too did old-style believers in the extrasensory perception**

> **of a "higher realm." Consider the opening lines spoken by Rod Serling on the late 1950s/early 1960s science-fiction TV series *The Twilight Zone:* There is a fifth dimension beyond that which is known to man. It is a dimension as vast as space and as timeless as infinity. It is the middle ground between light and shadow, between science and superstition, and it lies between the pit of man's fears and the summit of his knowledge. This is the dimension of imagination. It is an area which we call *The Twilight Zone.*[48]**

Even though many people used the science of the day to enhance their personal gain or deceive others for a profit, it did not change the fact that higher dimensions were a real possibility. Science was discovering that there is much more to the world than meets the eye. Perhaps angels were real, heaven is a real place, and God is the one that unifies everything. Science was advancing by answering long-asked questions about the universe and world. However, they were uncovering as many if not more questions in the process.

The foundation had been laid for talking about higher dimensions or extra dimensions without sounding crazy. The scientific world had opened a new opportunity for discussions that involved the unexplainable, the supernatural, or the multidimensional. Once quantum theory and string theory came onto the scene as a possible explanation for very weird occurrences at the subatomic level, science fiction and reality became even more exciting.

Chapter 4

Blown Minds and String Theory

Not only is the Universe stranger than we think, it is stranger than we can think.

–Werner Heisenberg, Across the Frontiers

Those who are not shocked when they first come across quantum theory cannot possibly have understood it.

–Niels Bohr, Essays 1932-1957 on Atomic Physics and Human Knowledge

Science made great strides in the twentieth century. Einstein had brought the world the theory of relativity, and space exploration had begun. Telescopes were seeing farther than ever before, and the galaxies were not only moving, but the universe was expanding. Scientists, as hard as they tried, could not find the edge of the universe. The universe they were able to see was huge. In fact, it was beyond huge. Chuck Missler uses an analogy to help one grasp the enormity of the universe. He writes:

The Sun is about 880,000 miles in diameter and it's about 93 million miles away from the Earth. If one inch represents the distance between the Earth and the Sun in our model, then the diameter of the Sun looks like a small dot—about a hundredth of an inch. All the planets of our solar system would then be able to fit within a five-foot circle. ... Our nearest solar neighbor is Alpha Centauri, a binary star system that is about twice the mass of our Sun. We are four and a

half light years away from Alpha Centauri. Using the same ratio for our model, the double-speck of Alpha Centauri hangs in the Universe about four and a half miles away from the speck of our Sun.[49]

The universe is big; in fact, it's bigger than most can imagine. But now science began opening a new door, the door to the "quantum" world. For most of history, scientists were studying the universe, nature, animals, plants, and objects that could be examined with the eyes, including with a microscope or telescope. With the advancements in technology and developments in discovering the fundamental forces, the door to the subatomic world was unlocked. Scientists became dedicated in their study of the tiny molecules, particles, and atoms. Gravity is an incredible force, but not at the quantum level. Magnetism can overcome the gravitational force. "At the scale of an atom, gravity is irrelevant compared to the electromagnetic force. In fact, a simple magnet can overcome the entire force of the planet Earth to pick up metallic objects, from paper clips to automobiles."[50] This scientific study was called quantum mechanics or quantum physics. Quantum is the world of the very, very small, and science was getting deeper and deeper into the quantum world.

Atoms

Even before the time of Christ, science has searched for the smallest element of a substance. If one were to cut an object in half, such as a peanut, and then cut it again, and again, what would the smallest unit of the peanut be? When would one get to the final, smallest element of the peanut? Democritus, a fifth-century Greek philosopher, "believed that you would eventually reach the smallest chunk of matter that couldn't be divided anymore, and [he] called these smallest chunks atoms."[51] Democritus' thinking was ahead of his time. The rest of the world would catch up much later when technology allowed scientists to examine the subatomic world. When they did, they discovered that materials are made up of microscopic particles that they appropriately called atoms. John Dalton, a chemist, was the first scientist to use the word *atom* to describe the basic unit of an element. He used the English word *atom* because the Greek word *atomos* that the philosopher Democritus introduced nearly 2,000 years prior means *indivisible*. "Dalton thought that the atom was the smallest unit of matter in the universe and could not be made smaller. In the 1890s the first subatomic particle, the electron, was found. This meant the atom was not the smallest unit of matter, though it kept its name in spite of this."[52]

Atoms are the fundamental pieces that make up everything in the known world. Atoms are different elements according to their structure. Atoms are made up of a nucleus of protons and neutrons stuck together, and electrons encompassing the nucleus.

The number of protons in the nucleus of an atom is what makes the atom a particular element on the periodic table. An element is a substance that cannot be broken down into simpler substances by chemical means. For instance, water can be broken down into hydrogen and oxygen atoms. But oxygen

> **cannot be broken down into any simpler compounds by chemical means. Therefore, oxygen is an element, water is not.**[53]

Carbon, nitrogen, gold, and hydrogen are all examples of atomic elements. Everything is made up of atoms: houses, computers, rocks, water, animals, people, everything. In the twentieth century, atoms were being studied and examined more intently than ever before by scientists. They wanted to find the smallest elements in the universe. Scientists were finding out that protons, neutrons, and electrons were not the most minor elements of an atom. Missler writes, "In recent years, we've learned that protons and neutrons are made of elementary particles called quarks. Electrons and neutrinos fall in the category of elementary particles called leptons. There's another category of elementary particles called bosons, the most familiar of which is the photon, the tiniest package of light."[54] Science was dissecting the atom in the hope of finding the smallest unit of matter.

Scientists also learned that atoms are almost entirely empty space. The nucleus of neutrons and protons is small and in the middle of the cloud of electrons. The space between the core and the outer shell is quite a large area comparatively speaking. The atoms are so small that the microscopic measurements make it difficult to understand just how roomy these atoms are. A comparison must be made to get the full picture. Missler writes, "So if we were going to build a model, we have an ambitious project. If we make the nucleus as big as a golf ball, our electron has to be three-quarters of a mile away. That's just the linear distance."[55] The volume of the nucleus as compared to the volume of the entire atom is just as impressive. "In other words, the nucleus of an atom has the same volume ratio to a full atom as one second does to 30 million years."[56] Atoms are mostly empty space, nothingness. This was first discovered by Ernest Rutherford as he worked with Niels Bohr.[57] (Though the Bohr model of an atom has been proven obsolete, the debate of whether an atom is empty space or solid matter remains.) When one looks around, they see solid materials—bricks, rocks, wood, houses, cars, concrete, etc. The human body is almost entirely empty space. Joseph Selbie in his book, *The Physics of God* states, "If all the space between the nucleus of the atoms and their orbiting electrons were removed, our bodies would be reduced to less than the size of a pinhead."[58] How can things be solid, if everything in the universe is mostly empty space? It goes back to the electromagnetic force holding the atoms together and maintaining the electrons in orbit. The fantastic force that atoms possess hold together everything in the universe.

Photons

Light is a wave, and light is a particle. One might say that's impossible, but in some equations, light functions as a wave, while in other equations, light functions as a particle. Light has been observed acting like a wave in various experiments. Therefore, light was believed to be a wave. But at other times, light behaved like particles or packets of energy. Discovering this duality of light was the beginning of quantum physics.

In 1900, a German physicist named Max Planck was searching for an explanation to a thermodynamics problem. "He resolved the problem by introducing a mathematical trick–if he assumed that energy was bundled in discrete packets, or quanta, the problem went away. It proved to be brilliant because it worked. There was no theoretical reason for doing this until Einstein came up with one five years later."[59]

The discovery that light acts in unexpected ways was a key to beginning to understand the quantum world. "Light, Einstein said, moved not in waves, but packets of energy. These packets of energy are called *photons*. Photons are one of the fundamental particles of physics that physicists hope to explain using string theory."[60] When scientists would work out formulas, light could act as a wave or a particle. When experiments were performed, light acted as a wave and a particle. Light had dual properties, and this became known as wave-particle duality. "This strange quantum behavior of particles and waves is crucial to understanding quantum theories, such as string theory."[61]

Another strange behavior of light is the intelligent-observer paradox. When experimenting to see if light was a wave or a particle, scientists discovered something interesting. Light acted like a particle when it was observed, but a wave when it was unobserved. The experiment consisted of shooting light through a double slit in a wall so that it would hit against a detector screen. As a wave, the light would spread out over the detector screen and create bands where the waves crisscrossed each other–much like water waves crisscrossing and spreading out against a sea wall. If the light hit the detector screen in two specific spots, like marbles being shot through the wall slits, then it would be particles. Scientists learned that the quantum world does strange things. When the double-slit experiment was performed, and individual photons or electrons were shot through the two slits against a detector screen, the pattern appeared as a wave. Even though the electrons were being shot individually, the result was as if waves were being shot through the slits. Missler adds:

> **Yet, even stranger, when the experimenters attempted to detect the electron as it passed through both slits, the electron decided to suddenly behave like a particle and choose one slit over the other. Because the experimenters tried to watch it, the electron created a bullet pattern on the detector—the kind made by particles. As long as nobody was trying to catch the electrons going through one slit or another, they created a wave interference pattern, but when experimenters tried to watch, the electrons created the bullet pattern of individual particles.**[62]

The intelligent-observer paradox brought another dynamic to the quantum world. The deeper scientists probed into the quantum world, the stranger things seemed. Does a conscious person watching the experiment change the wave to a particle? This paradox troubles many scientists because the answers are not clear and concise. Some accept this as weird science and move on. Others like Joseph Selbie firmly believe that a person's consciousness plays a role in determining the outcome of the wave or particle.

> **Physicists have gone on to prove, thousands of times, that until measured by an intelligent observer,**

> **everything—whether energy such as light, or matter such as atoms—behaves in a wavelike manner until measured by an intelligent observer. The inescapable conclusion: *An intelligent observer plays an essential role in the formation of matter.*[63]**

That means nothing appears as a particle until a person observes it. The notion sounds crazy and unbelievable as a scientific position. But that is what some scientists believe, including Niels Bohr (1885-1962), who is considered the father of quantum physics. "[Bohr] was among the first to conclude that physical objects do not have an independent, objective reality. He stated categorically that physical objects appear only when we observe them—and his assertion has never been disproven."[64] Another noted scientist goes on the record:

> **Jon von Neuman (1903-1957), who is considered to be one of the greatest mathematicians of the 20th century and who was also a scientist on the Manhattan Project, asserts that consciousness doesn't merely affect reality; consciousness *creates* reality. And as counterintuitive as it may seem, von Neumann's views also rest on rigorous mathematics.[65]**

Another possible answer is that light makes the choice, not the observer.

> **The observer effect doesn't mean that someone can look at an electron and collapse it to a particle. The machines that observed and measured the particles in the double-slit experiments used beams of light within the electromagnetic radiation spectrum. As the particles were observed and measured by use of light beams, they transitioned into a localized particle, writes Dennis Zetting.[66]**

The photon or light is the key to the intelligent-observer paradox according to Zetting. "Although some people claim that consciousness or human observation can cause waves to collapse into particles, light is the only proven transitioning agent known to science that will transition particles from the non-local realm (wave state) into the local realm (particle state)..."[67]

Another extraordinary finding for scientists was quantum entanglement.

> **It was discovered that particles could come in "entangled" pairs. If the spin of one entangled particle was up, the other one always had a down spin, even when they were separated by a significant distance. They behaved as though they were in instant communication, no matter how far they were apart.**[68]

Scientists were suggesting, as strange as it sounds, that particles were communicating with each other. Many experiments were done to prove or disprove quantum entanglement, also known as nonlocality, and time and time again, it was proven to be true. Missler writes this of an experiment:

> **[Dr. Alain] Aspect and his team heated cesium atoms using lasers, which sent two photons travelling in opposite directions through six-and-a-half meters of pipe to special polarization analyzers. The photons communicated in 10 nanoseconds, 30 nanoseconds less than information could have crossed the 13 meters between them at light speed. The researchers showed directly that paired photons are "nonlocal." They don't act on their own like independent agents, free to do whatever they want on their own side of the pipe. They are tied to their partner in a way that implies faster-than-light-speed intimacy. In fact, every particle in the universe seems to be connected**

> **to every other. These are astonishing discoveries that should up-end everything we think about what is "real." The very nature of our universe comes into question.[69]**

Trying to explain nonlocality was so tricky that one prevalent theory, the Copenhagen interpretation, simply suggested, "that is the way it is, don't try and understand it, just accept it."[70] David Bohm, a physicist, a fellow of England's prestigious Royal Society, and writer of the 1951 book entitled *Quantum Theory* chose not to accept the Copenhagen interpretation. "Bohm instead embraced the fact of nonlocality, accepted its counterintuitive down-the-rabbit-hole implications, and set out to understand what it could mean. He came to the conclusion—startling but inescapable mathematically—that the entire cosmos is one continuous interconnected whole."[71]

Atoms were being broken down into smaller and smaller parts. Light or photons had strange qualities that impacted the universe and other particles. The intelligent-observer paradox added a new dynamic to the already strange discoveries. Quantum entanglement or nonlocality was like icing on the quantum cake. The more in-depth scientists dug into the quantum world, the more confusing things became instead of more transparent. Scientists wanted to make things cleaner and neater, not messier and fuzzier. String theory came on the scene to unify these crazy findings and understand what in the world (or universe) was going on. However, in order to bring unity to the quantum world, more strangeness would be added in terms of dimensions.

String Theory

String theory came about as a result of complicated processes by scientists to unify the theory of relativity with quantum theory. "String theory's main idea is that all of the subatomic particles in quantum physics are actually made of much smaller vibrating strands of energy. The strings can vibrate from left to right, or right to left, and the different ways they vibrate determines the kind of particle they create."[72] The theory suggests that the smallest unit of anything, the most basic unit of a particle, is a vibrating string. That would mean that tiny vibrating strings of energy would be at the core of everything in the universe, of all matter. The vibrations of the strings determine the kind of particle they are, while the particles determine what kind of atom they are. The mathematics is very in-depth and complicated, but for string theory to work, it must have multiple dimensions of space.

The various dimensions of space have been an enormous roadblock to many scientists getting onboard with the theory. Over time, string theory has developed and progressed instead of falling apart and fading away. More and more scientists have cautiously accepted string theory as plausible. The string theory equations seem to move towards a unification of gravity and electromagnetism. "The closed strings of string theory correspond to the behavior expected for gravity. Specifically, they have properties that match the long-sought-after *graviton*, a particle that would carry the force of gravity between objects."[73]

The extra dimensions needed for string theory to be true is what makes this theory so fascinating and popular. Many people have heard of string theory even though they probably do not know what it is. The road leading to string theory has been paved with the strange and weird but seemingly true wave-particle duality, quantum entanglement or nonlocality, and the intelligent-observer paradox. Taking another step towards extra dimensions does not seem as far out after contemplating all the quantum craziness. George Musser writes:

> **Blown minds are an occupational hazard in string theory, never more so than when talking about one of the theory's most distinctive aspects: extra dimensions of space. ... String theory suggests that space has a total of nine dimensions—six more than the ones we see. M-theory, which underlies string theory, adds yet one more. Including time, that makes a total of eleven.**[74]

String theory needs more than three spatial dimensions in order to work. The point of this book is to show that science points to higher dimensions or more spatial dimensions than the mere three in which humans live. Therefore, seeing higher dimensions in the Bible is not an imaginative stretch. Musser, however, does explain why ten spatial dimensions are needed:

> **Why would space have 10 dimensions rather than, say, 42? In 10-D space, string theory is able to marry all the particle dynasties together. The electron pairs off with a sibling of the photon, which in turn finds itself related to more exotic particles. The end result is one big happy family. If there were fewer than 10 dimensions, particles would split into isolated clans. If there were more than 10, the family would admit**

some black sheep—additional particles that refused to interact with the others. Either all particles must interact, or none can, so the presence of a few antisocial particles would force all the other particles to cease interacting as well.[75]

String theory needs extra spatial dimensions for the unification of forces to work. These extra spatial dimensions (if string theory is correct) could be another piece pointing to a higher spiritual dimension as seen in the Bible. Are these the dimensions where one would find angels or heaven? The fact that scientists are okay with higher dimensions opens the door for seeing the spiritual dimensions in the Bible as more than myth or fantasy. A key challenge with aligning the spiritual realm with the higher dimensions envisioned by string theory is that there are options for the nature and location of these extra dimensions. Jones and Robbins write:

Two possible explanations currently exist for the location of the extra dimensions:

[1] The extra space dimensions (generally six of them) are curled up (*compactified*, in string terminology) to incredibly small sizes, so we never perceive them.

[2] We are stuck on a three-dimensional brane, and the extra dimensions extend off of it and are inaccessible to us.[76]

The thought of extra dimensions extending from man's three spatial dimensions clearly opens a door to envisioning a vast spiritual realm immediately adjacent to the visible world. Is it possible that as science searches for the beginning of the universe, that they are finding evidence for God and a spiritual dimension? As science digs deeper into the subatomic world, they come closer to God whether they realize it or not. Is it possible that humans were designed to live in three dimensions of space and one dimension of time, but their perception into the higher dimensions was marred by sin and the fall? As science teeters on the edge of discovering the spiritual dimensions that have been hidden from people, they are receiving overwhelming evidence that there is more to life than meets the eye.

Bernard Haisch writes:

> **It is acceptable today, even fashionable, to publish scientific papers that propound theories of indivisible universes that may be adjacent to our own in other dimensions. ...If a religious person talks about transcendent spiritual realities he or she is scoffed at. For some reason, the eleven or twenty-six-dimensional string worlds of scientific theory are plausible, but the supernatural realms of mysticism are judged to be mere superstition.**[77]

Dark Matter & Dark Energy

Dark matter and dark energy are possible scientific discoveries that point to the reality of a higher dimension. Dark matter is the product of scientists examining the effects of the force of gravity in the universe. They noticed that the outer portions of a galaxy were spinning just as fast as the inner parts of the galaxy, but they were not falling apart or being slung into other galaxies. Everything spins at the same speed and holds together perfectly. “The galaxies should be flying apart if the outsides are moving so fast."[78] For example, if a person were to stand on a giant, oversized merry-go-round in a schoolyard playground that is spinning at a consistent speed, the force near the middle of the merry-go-round is much less than the force on the outer part of the merry-go-round. It is easier to hang on near the middle. It is much more difficult to hang on near the edge. Nola Taylor Redd writes:

> **Astronomers examining spiral galaxies in the 1950s expected to see material in the center moving faster than on the outer edges. Instead, they found the stars in both locations traveled at the same velocity, indicating the galaxies contained more mass than could be seen. Studies of the gas within elliptical galaxies also indicated a need for more mass than found in visible objects. Clusters of galaxies would fly apart if the only mass they contained were visible to conventional astronomical measurements.**[79]

Dark matter is a mysterious, unseen "thing" that has enough mass to hold the galaxies together. Science postulates that since much of a galaxy is empty space, there must be additional mass located within the galaxy that keeps it from flying apart. Scientists can calculate the missing mass based on observed behavior, but no matter can be seen with human eyes.

Today, scientists are generally assuming that dark matter holds the galaxies together and keeps them from falling to pieces, and dark energy pushes the giant galaxies further from each other, creating an expansion of the universe. Albert Einstein led the way for many scientists in believing that the universe was static, that it could not be expanding. However, with the invention of the Hubble telescope, which allows scientists to see galaxies, and more scientific attention being given to calculations, the consensus was soon reached that the universe is expanding. Scientists also thought that the expanding universe had to be a result of the Big Bang. If that were the case, they thought the expansion would be steady or possibly even slowing down. Chuck Missler writes, "Researchers were surprised to find that neither scenario appeared to be taking place. Instead, they saw that the universe was not just continuing to expand, but it was doing so at a faster and faster rate. ...The accelerated expansion of the universe is blamed on another mysterious source of force called *dark energy*."[80] There must be energy in the universe that is pushing the galaxies apart. Scientists call this "dark energy."

The dark matter and dark energy postulated by scientists are significant factors in the universe used to explain the seemingly unexplainable. As with other forces, they are detectable but not visible. Could dark matter and dark energy be further scientific insights pointing towards higher spatial dimensions? For that matter, could dark matter and dark energy be pointing mankind to where the spiritual dimension is located? Perhaps science is finding the spiritual dimension as they discover invisible matter and energy that make up ninety-five percent of the universe. Coby Bartolucci, a Christian who aspires to be an astrophysicist one day, is merely speculating when he states:

> **In the Bible, Heaven and Hell are depicted as places that one can never physically reach in our universe. At this point, most people probably think they're just entirely separate from the world we know—that each is not a physical dimension at all, but rather some type of spiritual realm. But, what if they are physical?**

> **What if those other universes that scientists are postulating are actually the universe that exists as Heaven and another that is Hell?**[81]

The spiritual dimension may be where unseen dark matter and energy reside in the three-dimensional universe. If heaven has dimensionality and locality just as the Bible describes, then maybe the missing matter in the universe is where heaven is located. Though it cannot be seen, its mass impacts the present universe in a way that suggests something more is there but is still hidden to the three-dimensional person.

It is possible that the spiritual realm or higher dimension intersects the three-dimensional world in such way that its mass and energy are detectable through gravity and the bending of light. Scientists are detecting the bending of light around large objects in the universe. The problem is, they cannot see the objects around which the light is bending. The matter is not visible. Missler states:

> **Dark matter is also useful for explaining an effect called "gravitational lensing," caused when light has to warp around large celestial objects. Astronomers will observe the light from a single galaxy coming at us several different times in different locations because that light had to go around a large object in space. The light had to have warped around this object on different sides, thus coming to us as several images of the same galaxy. Dark matter is credited as the cause of this warping of light in space.**[82]

The light is warping around something; some object with mass is affecting the light. Could it be a higher dimension? Could it be that the spiritual dimension where heaven is located and where angels live is so close to the three-dimensional world, science is now receiving a clue to its existence? It is very possible.

Many-worlds Interpretation and Parallel Universes

Many of the results scientists were discovering in the quantum world were difficult to explain. One of the biggest was the intelligent-observer paradox. A wave could be a particle, and a particle could be a wave. It merely depended on whether or not an intelligent observer was watching. To resolve the apparent conflict or paradox, scientists proposed various answers. One answer was the many-worlds interpretation: "... *the many worlds interpretation (MWI)* of Hugh Everett III proposes that the wavefunction never actually collapses, but all possibilities become actualities—just in alternate realities. The universe is continually splitting apart as every quantum question is resolved in every possible way across an immense multiverse of parallel universes."[83]

The basis for this theory is that there are two possibilities for the photon, wave or particle. Before the photon is observed, it exists in both states. If the photon exists in both states, would it be possible that there are two universes, each containing the opposite reality? In one universe, the photon would be a wave, and in the other universe the photon would be a particle.

> **Everett arrived at this theory in part by taking the mathematics of quantum theory and assuming it could be taken literally. If the equation shows that there are two possibilities, then why not assume that there are two possibilities? When you look inside**

the box, instead of something odd happening to the quantum system, you actually become part of the quantum system. You now exist in two states.[84]

The point of this section is not to explain and dissect the many-worlds interpretation. The purpose is to show how very intelligent scientists can propose and believe as a plausible theory the many-worlds interpretation while at the same time discounting the possibility of a spiritual realm and a God who could have created the universe and all that it contains.

Variations of the many-worlds interpretation exist. Jones and Robbins write, "The *multiverse* is a theory in which our universe is not the only one, but states that many universes exist parallel to each other. These distinct universes within the multiverse theory are called parallel universes. A variety of different theories lend themselves to a multiverse viewpoint."[85] One MIT cosmologist, Max Tegmark, proposes four levels of parallel universes. These four levels are presented in both *String Theory for Dummies* and *The Complete Idiots' Guide to String Theory*.

Scientists are continually uncovering evidence that suggests the strong possibility of a spiritual dimension. Scientists are discovering over and over again that there is much more to the universe and life than meets the eye. The deeper scientists get into the minute details of God's creation, the more confounded they become and the more they resort to incredibly imaginative theories for answers because they refuse to acknowledge a higher power, a designer who made everything. Dennis Zetting, a Christian scientist and author, proposes that the many-worlds interpretation should include God since that is one of the infinite possibilities. He writes:

> **According to this model God is not only a possibility but God would be proven to exist. Since there is nothing in science that proves God cannot or does not exist, and the many-worlds interpretation claims that every possible universe exists, then there are universes that must have God. In addition, if there are universes that have God, then there is a magnitude (possibly an infinite) number of universes with God.[86]**

From the theory of relativity to parallel universes, science opened the door to new and exciting possibilities. For the one who believes that God created the universe and has an active role and relationship with His creation, science is discovering more and more about the creator of the universe. With string theory proposing six more dimensions than people previously knew and the quantum world bringing more philosophical questions than tangible answers, it is no longer either unusual or irrational to believe in the spiritual dimension. The more scientists discover, the more evidence they uncover that suggests a creator exists. The more people inspect the creation, the more they learn about the creator. It appears most scientists are just not open to that possibility, in this universe at least.

Chapter 5

Living in a Designer World

Why do I believe in God? As a physicist, I look at nature from a particular perspective. I see an orderly, beautiful universe in which nearly all physical phenomena can be understood from a few simple mathematical equations. I see a universe that, had it been constructed slightly differently, would never have given birth to stars and planets, let alone bacteria and people. And there is no good scientific reason for why the universe should not have been different.

–William D. Phillips, a Nobel Laureate in physics

I find it quite improbable that such order came out of chaos. There has to be some organizing principle. God, to me, is a mystery but is the explanation for the miracle of existence, why there is something instead of nothing.

–Allan Sandage (1926-2010), winner of the Crawford Prize in Astronomy whose research led him to become a Christian at the age of 50

If the evidence demonstrates that someone created the universe, then there must be a higher dimension or spiritual realm. The only possibility for a creator to create at least three dimensions of space and at least one dimension of time is to be outside of all the dimensions He created. If the creator is outside of space and time, He is in a higher dimension some place, outside of the dimensions He created. Proving a creator proves, at the very least, a higher dimension where the creator resides.

Someone once said, "You can't see the forest for the trees." The meaning of this expression is, sometimes people get so focused on the little things or get so close to that which they are examining, that they miss the big picture. Many people, and especially scientists, get so focused on the parts of the universe, or man, or atoms and molecules that they do not see the big picture. Bernard Haisch writes,

> **The epistemology of science is built on the assumption that we live in a physical universe comprised of matter and energy whose workings can be understood by reducing them to their most basic components: molecules, atoms, quarks, and perhaps, ultimately even superstrings. In short, it assumes a universe that can be taken apart like a watch to see what makes it tick. This is the universe of reductionism—a universe in which everything can be reduced to the behavior of particles of matter and energy.**[87]

Sometimes scientists can get so focused on the individual parts of the watch, that they forget there must have been a watchmaker who put it all together. Haisch says that scientists assume they can take apart the universe and find out how it was initially made. The mere fact that people can sit down at a desk and type out a paper on a computer about contemplating their existence is astonishing. The sun, moon, and stars are incredible. The way the human body functions, the nature of atoms, mathematics, a person's consciousness, languages, and communication mediums of various kinds all point to something greater than chance. John von Neumann, a physicist and mathematician, said, "There probably is a God. Many things are easier to explain if there is than if there isn't."[88] Still, most scientists do not like to add God to any of their theories, even though doing so would be logical.

Most American scientists believe in God much less frequently than other sectors of the United States population. In May and June of 2009, the Pew Research Center for the People & the Press showed that while ninety-five percent of the general public believed in God or a higher power of some kind, only fifty-one percent of scientists believed in God or some kind of higher power.[89] Some scientists believe in God or a spiritual being of some sort, but few believe in the God of the Bible. (Several scientists are Christians, including Dennis Zetting, who is quoted in this book. He is a member of the American Scientific Affiliation of over 2,000 members.)[90]

Scientists like to test things. They like to do experiments and study the results. From their results, laws and principles are discovered that govern the universe and the world in which people live. Science shows people what the world and universe are like and how it functions presently. As scientists search for how everything began, they move into theoretical science. They make assumptions or educated guesses based upon present evidence. However, they seek answers that do not involve God. The Bible clearly teaches that God created everything. The method scientists have chosen has no laws or principles to guide them in accepting that truth.

A Christian will accept the truth of Scripture and look to further understand or affirm th at tr uth wi th ev idence from

God's world and universe. The problem with the scientist looking backwards using the present universal laws is that when Adam and Eve sinned, some laws may have been impacted or completely changed. According to the Scriptures, a significant difference exists between the perfect original creation and the present blemished universe. This chapter seeks to briefly look at some of the evidence that God created the universe and all that is within it. This is not meant to be an exhaustive list. A few topics are chosen that scientists might find in their search for a theory of everything or the search for the beginning of the universe.

Order in the Universe

If science points to higher dimensions and God dwells in higher dimensions of space and time, then the laws and principles guiding God may be more complex than the laws and principles that govern the three-dimensional space and one dimension of time from which man observes. Since the Bible teaches that the spiritual realm is real, trying to solve the beginning of the universe without considering the spiritual realm would be flawed and shortsighted. The fact that science is pointing to the possibility of additional dimensions is evidence for the possibility of a grand designer who created the three-dimensional realm.

The universe is vast and has order and laws that govern its expanding space. Since no one (but God) was around when everything began, no one can know for sure what happened in the beginning. Whether a person believes God created the universe and all that is in it, or that everything happened by random chance, a measure of faith is required for both. For the believer, there is faith that God is speaking the truth in His Word. The faith is that God's Word is true based upon God's record of being true throughout the Bible. For the unbeliever, it is faith in a theory or idea that is based upon the intelligence and academic integrity of the theorists. There is a faith that God spoke and everything came into being as a result. There is also a faith that a big bang happened, and billions of years later, there are millions of different plants, animals and people. It takes faith to believe either of these scenarios.

Many scientists, and people for that matter, do not even give creation a chance because they think it to be impossible. It is quite remote in possibilities, but so is evolution. The possibility that the technological world in which mankind lives today evolved from matter that has no life within itself is close to zero. Amir D. Aczel held a master's degree in science and a Ph.D. in mathematics. He authored several books, including *Why Science Does Not Disprove God.* In a *Time* magazine article, Aczel wrote:

> **The great British mathematician Roger Penrose has calculated—based on only one of the hundreds of parameters of the physical universe—that the probability of the emergence of a life-giving cosmos was 1 divided by 10, raised to the power 10, and again raised to the power of 123. This is a number as close to zero as anyone has ever imagined. (The probability is much, much smaller than that of winning the Mega Millions jackpot for more days than the universe has been in existence.)**[91]

The odds that the earth and all of its inhabitants are here from a huge explosion billions of years ago is beyond astronomically low. The alternative is a grand designer or divine programmer that created all of this. Some scientists do recognize the consistency between belief in God and science itself. Scientist Haisch cites an article from *U.S. News and World Report* entitled, "What Came Before Creation?"

> **Other natural constants that trace back to the big bang also seem strangely fine-tuned in favor of a universe amenable to consciousness. Had gravity been only slightly stronger, stars would burn through their nuclear fuel in less than a year: life could never evolve, much less settle in. Had the strong force that holds the nucleus of atoms together been only slightly weaker, stars could never have formed. So far, no theory is even close to explaining why physical laws exist, much less why they take the form they do. Standard big-bang theory, for example, essentially explains the propitious universe in this way: "Well, we got lucky."**[92]

The precision and orderliness in the universe are also evidence for a grand designer. Haisch believes in a big bang, but he also believes that someone must have directed the big bang and its subsequent happenings. He believes someone is behind all of this. The laws that suspend planets in space and the motion happening among planetary bodies within the universe points to someone or something more significant than the universe itself. Paul Davies writes, "The most striking and successful application of Newton's mechanics was to the motion of the planets in the solar system. Thus the music of the spheres was replaced by the image of the clockwork universe. God the

Geometer became God the Watchmaker."[93] The universe does not appear to be the result of an explosion. It seems to be the result of a finely tuned universe maker. The laws in the universe seem to point to a higher being or designer. Paul Davies is a British-born theoretical physicist, cosmologist, astrobiologist and best-selling author. He lists four reasons that the laws of the universe point to God:

- **First and foremost, the laws are universal. ...The laws are taken to apply unfailingly everywhere in the universe and at all epochs of cosmic history.**

- **Second, the laws are absolute. They do not depend on anything else.**

- **Third and most important, the property of the laws of nature: they are eternal. The timeless, eternal character of the laws is reflected in the mathematical structure employed to model the physical world.**

- **Fourth, the laws are omnipotent. By this, I mean that nothing escapes them; they are all-powerful.**[94]

Anthropic Principle

The anthropic principle is the theory that the earth's place in the universe is positioned in the perfect location for life, particularly human life. *Merriam-Webster* defines the anthropic principle as follows: "Either of two principles in cosmology: a) conditions that are observed in the universe must allow the observer to exist—called also *weak anthropic principle.* b) the universe must have properties that make inevitable the existence of intelligent life—called also *strong anthropic principle*."[95]

The earth is just the right distance from the sun, and its tilt is perfect for the seasons. The atmosphere and ozone are balanced perfectly. Chuck Missler writes, "If we were closer to the sun, we'd be too warm to maintain a stable water cycle, and the water would evaporate away. If we were further from the sun, our water would be locked in ice year-round."[96] The various forces are balanced just right for life on the planet Earth. Gravity is not too strong, but not too weak. Even Earth's crust and magnetic field seem to be designed perfectly. Missler says Earth's magnetic field is an incredible protector for the lives that inhabit the planet. He says that if Earth's magnetic field "were stronger, we would suffer the powerful electromagnetic storms that are found on the surfaces of the larger planets. If it were weaker, we'd be exposed to a greater beating from stellar radiation. As it is, the magnetic field diverts dangerous space particles away from the planet's surface by pushing them out and around it."[97] So many things have to be just right for life to exist on Earth that the odds are once again astronomical that people are here and contemplating their existence by random chance.

The structure of atoms and the molecular world are evidence of a grand designer. The energy that sustains every atom in the universe is massive. A relatively small set of elements make up the matter found in the universe. The way atoms interact to make up molecules, and the way molecules form compounds indicate that everything in the world is finely tuned. "Everything we observe from plant life, stars, animals, rocks, air, and water—virtually everything—is composed of 90 naturally occurring building blocks known as atoms. ...God's organization of the universe can be seen in the smallest unit of substance, the atom," writes Craig A. Perman, a Christian who holds a master's degree in chemistry. He continues, "They are the fundamental building blocks of all materials. Atoms are not chaotic in their assembly but have an orderly arrangement in the way that electrons are added to orbitals, and protons and neutrons in the nucleus. This accounts for their periodic and predictable attributes which a God of order has created."[98]

Entropy

Explosions do not create order and unity through random chance. They disorganize and disrupt. Explosions have never brought order by chance. The second law of thermodynamics is well known in the scientific world, as well as the non-scientific world, even if the average person cannot state the law. Gerard J. Keane, a Christian believer, writes:

> **The behavioral tendency of matter is always in a *downward* direction, never *upward* in the absence of any programming (e.g., coded machinery such as characterizes living things.) Without such programming, matter does not transform itself into higher and higher levels of organization. For example, buildings and equipment always tend to deteriorate unless maintained adequately. Another example: Heat will only flow from a hot object to a cold object, until a temperature equilibrium is reached in both.**[99]

Entropy is the scientific term for the disorder that happens with the arrow of time and is the benchmark of the second law of thermodynamics. "The term *entropy* measures the degree of disorder. All natural changes take place so that the entropy increases. As a result, the entropy of the universe is constantly increasing."[100] Entropy points to the fact that everything around us was once more orderly than it is now. The universe is getting more disorganized, not more organized. This is clear evidence for a grand designer that created the universe with order, not an explosion that caused order. Even secular scientists who would never accept creation from a biblical perspective see the progression from order to disorder. "Why is entropy always increasing? The reason is actually simple: If there's one right way to put something together, there are many wrong ways to do it," writes Carlos Calle, a senior research analyst at NASA. He continues:

> **For example, if you pick up all the pieces of a jigsaw puzzle that you accidentally dropped on the floor and quickly put them right side up on the table, you don't expect the puzzle to be put together the right way. There is only one correct way to put the pieces together and very many incorrect ways. Chances are you won't put them together the right way the first time.[101]**

The secular scientists' very argument from the law of entropy for order not coming from chaos is the exact reason to believe in a grand designer of the universe and not a universal accident.

According to the second law of thermodynamics (entropy), the universe is winding down; it's cooling off and slowing down. The universe will eventually reach an evenly distributed temperature. "Cosmologists call this the 'heat death' of the universe, an inevitable consequence of the unstoppable march of entropy."[102] Basic logic, using the laws of thermodynamics, suggests that there was a time when everything began in a more organized state than the present. The Bible teaches that God created the universe with order. Genesis 1:14 says, "Then God said, 'Let there be lights in the firmament of the heavens to divide the day from the night; and let them be for signs and seasons, and for days and years.'" Verse 18 of the same Bible chapter continues, "...and God saw that it was good." God claims that He created the universe perfect and with order. Because of the way God made the universe or because of sin, the law of entropy was introduced. Missler points to entropy being a result of sin.

> **We suspect that there is a relationship between entropy and the Fall. Adam and Eve were able to live forever until they disobeyed God and sin entered the world, "and death by sin." There's a number of us that suspect that the entropy laws were introduced under the curse. In Romans 8, Paul tells us that the entire creation is subject to the "bondage of decay" and that one day it will be set free, just like we are. The day will come when the curse is fully repealed, and that will be an exciting day. The entropy laws are limited, and they too will end.**[103]

Entropy leads one to believe that things are getting worse, not better. The universe and everything in it had a starting point, and everything began in a good state. For that to be possible, a grand designer must have made everything. If a grand designer made everything, He must be outside of the three-dimensional world.

A Person's Consciousness

Consciousness is more than mere brain activity. Brain functionality is incredibly amazing. The human brain is essentially a computer made of living cells and connected to a body. The brain is the central guidance system of the human body. However, consciousness is a bit deeper and more profound than just brain activity. David Chalmers, who holds a Ph.D. in philosophy and cognitive science, spoke at the University of Arizona about consciousness. When speaking about the "only one truly hard problem of consciousness," Chalmers said:

> **It's this: why on earth should all those complicated brain processes feel like anything from the inside? Why aren't we just brilliant robots, capable of retaining information, of responding to noises and smells and hot saucepans, but dark inside, lacking an inner life? And how does the brain manage it? How could the 1.4 kg lump of moist, pinkish-beige tissue inside your skull give rise to something as mysterious as the experience of being that pinkish-beige lump, and the body to which it is attached?**[104]

For scientists that believe in only the material world, consciousness is more difficult to explain. For the scientists that believe in a divine being or in God, the consciousness is a person's spirit, the eternal part of a person. Haisch gives the three primary views of consciousness:

- **The first holds that the material world is all there is. In this view, everything can ultimately be reduced to physics and nothing but physics. Reality is nothing more than space, time, particles, and forces that physicists document.**

- **The second view of consciousness holds that material reality is primary, but not exclusive. In this view, something greater than material reality has arisen out of ordinary matter through some kind of complex evolutionary process. ... The survival of consciousness after death is, therefore, also deemed unlikely.**

- **The third view of consciousness holds that material reality is not only non-exclusive; it is secondary. Something else came first. ...The brain is, indeed, a data processor, but intelligence and consciousness reside elsewhere. The ability of consciousness to exist apart from the body and to survive death is, therefore, likely.**[105]

The fact that most people contemplate their own future after their death is not only amazing, but it points to the possibility of a person's consciousness living on after the body dies. Nearly every society, people group, or person considers life after death. People did not evolve into their consciousness. It was built into them. Several scientists have studied Near Death Experiences (NDEs) trying to prove life after death is a fact from a scientific standpoint. One such scientist is Emily Williams Kelly. An article entitled, "Beyond Death: The Science of the Afterlife," by *Time* magazine is an interview with Kelly about her studies. Kelly's very credible and distinguished education from the Universities of Virginia, Duke, and Edinburgh are highlighted. Lisa Miller, the article's author, says Kelly has spent her career researching, as she puts it, "the interface between the brain and the mind."[106] Those who study NDEs have the difficult task of documenting the experiences of dying people, of people who momentarily die and then are brought back, and people who have been in comas. The idea is documenting a person's conscious experience when the brain seems to be essentially stopped and finding commonalities in their experiences. "If our conscious experience totally depends on the brain, then there can't be an afterlife—when the brain is gone, the mind is gone. But it's not that simple. Even when the brain seems to be virtually disabled, people are still having these experiences," says Kelly.[107] The article continues, "What is she saying? That upon death, people really go to another realm? And that science can prove it? Kelly shrugs. NDEs 'tell us to open our minds and think there may be a great deal more to mind and consciousness—that's as far as I'm willing to go.'"[108] NDEs may not prove an afterlife, but they are another small piece that points to a spiritual dimension. The fact that a person has the mental ability to ponder their consciousness and believe that life is more than a physical, three-dimensional body possibly points to a spiritual realm to which a person's soul also belongs. People are preprogrammed with a consciousness or soul, and consideration of afterlife is a result of that very truth.

To believe in evolution and see the various types and kinds of living beings is to wonder why some evolved into frogs and others into birds, while others evolved into humans—humans that can now reason, think, write, build computers and robots, etc. Where are all the "in-between" species? Where are all the missing links in the evolutionary chain? If evolution is true, there must have been millions of these missing links just between primates and humans. Why did some of the animals remain primates while others evolved into humans? Why is there such a huge intellectual gap between primates and humans? The human race's superior brain abilities to reason, think, and learn sets them apart from the animal kingdom by a great distance. But it is the consciousness that takes it to a much higher level. Haisch writes:

> **Biologists today struggle with the profound problem of forging an evolutionary chain between the inanimate primordial soup and thinking human beings. For neuroscientists, the challenge is to discover how the brain and its chemistry gave rise to consciousness. ...The mystics...point in the opposite direction. Matter does not create consciousness; they tell us consciousness creates matter.**[109]

Many will point to the intelligent-observer paradox (introduced in chapter four) to theorize that a person's consciousness plays a role in the existence of the universe.

Purpose

Another piece of evidence that points to a designer or creator of all things is purpose. Do people have a purpose? Is there more to life than being born, living, and then dying? The materialist will answer the questions by saying no. That leaves many in the scientific world wondering why they should work so hard and whether their life's work matters in the end. Haisch writes:

> **Let's face it. The reductionist view of human destiny is bleak. I am constantly baffled by the fact that a majority of my colleagues seem to prefer a philosophical view of human beings as short-lived, chemically-driven machines that evolved by accident in a random, remote corner of the universe and**

whose existence is a pointless and utterly transient curiosity.[110]

The Bible clearly gives mankind's purpose as having a relationship with the creator of the universe. Mankind's purpose is to worship and serve God, to be dependent upon God in all things. Though sin messed up this purpose, God, through Jesus Christ, allowed the relationship to be restored. Even unbelieving people battle within themselves about the sense of meaning and purpose. Rick Warren, pastor of Saddleback Church in California, wrote a book called *Purpose Driven Life* in 2002. The book has sold more than thirty million copies.[111] It has also been translated into more languages than any other book except the Bible and was on the *New York Times* best-seller list four straight years.[112]

It is interesting that several unbelieving scientists are awakening to the reality of a creator. Many of the books written by scientists, read by this author in preparation for writing this book, seem to point to some kind of higher being who created life or at least initiated the evolution of the universe. Something draws these scientists to believe that people are not here by chance; everything is too coincidental to have just happened. If people are not here by chance, then there must be more to life than living and dying. The temporary life from random chance encourages selfishness. Selfishness becomes the primary motivator in a person's life as a result. If this life is all there is, then the quality and quantity of one's life is of utmost importance. What does that do to people who have a seemingly poor quality of life in this view? Some who embrace this view often see very poor people, people who are mentally challenged or physically handicapped and thus unable to enjoy life fully as people who should just end their lives and be put out of their misery. That is where a reductionist view of life leads to seeing human beings as temporary organisms. If everyone dies and that is it—no memory, no consciousness, no afterlife—then abortion, euthanasia, and mercy killings of various kinds are all reasonable options.

Paul Davies sees something more than an accident when he looks at the universe and all that is in it. He writes:

> **I belong to the group of scientists who do not subscribe to a conventional religion but nevertheless deny that the universe is a purposeless accident. Through my scientific work I have come to believe more and more strongly that the physical universe is put together with an ingenuity so astonishing that I cannot accept it merely as a brute fact. There must, it seems to me, be a deeper level of explanation.**[113]

Many agree with Paul Davies that there must be something more to life than matter and the universe must be more than an accident. If that is true, a supreme being is behind all of this, and He must be outside of man's three spatial dimensions in a higher spatial dimension. That realization would point to the conclusion that the spiritual realm is that higher dimension.

Chapter 6

The Digital 3-D Program Called "Life"

The exquisite order displayed by our scientific understanding of the physical world calls for the divine.

–Vera Kistiakowsky, MIT physicist

There is no subject in space-time without a conscious subject looking at it.

–Amit Goswami, quantum physicist

If man is living in a digital universe, then digitally created higher dimensions or a spiritual realm is a great probability. Just as the creator and builder of a computer must be more advanced than his creation—the computer and its programming—the creator of the universe and all that is within it must be much more intelligent and considerably more advanced than His creation—humans and the world we inhabit.

The foundation has already been laid for a higher dimensional universe where a person inhabits only three of its spatial dimensions and one dimension of time. God creates the universe and all the matter in it, then places within man a consciousness or eternal spirit. The world is made up of tiny elements, atoms, which are the building blocks for everything. Different combinations of these atoms make different materials. As stated in chapter four, the strange truth about atoms is, they consist of mostly empty space. That means, all matter is almost entirely space; matter is not solid. It is as if God made everything to appear solid, but it is an illusion.

Even those who do not believe in God realize that the world is not as it seems. The quantum world was supposed to lead scientists to more answers, but it led instead to more questions. The world of atoms, electrons, and photons unlocked the door to confusing reality and the imaginary. Quantum theory introduced the idea that the universe and the physical world are digital. George Musser states:

> **The world is digital. Many essential properties of nature are discrete—that is, they come in distinct units, like bytes of computer memory or pixels on a screen. For instance, matter consists of particles. Particles' properties are often restricted to a limited number of allowed values. Even when properties can take on a continuous range of values, they are restricted in other ways.**[114]

As science seeks to find a solid and material answer, the more clues they find that point to the spiritual realm. The closer they get to a solution, the closer they get to God.

The Intelligent-Observer Paradox

The point when scientists began to question reality is when quantum science developed the intelligent-observer theory (introduced and explained in chapter four). If the determining factor of changing a wave into a particle is an intelligent observer, then matter does not exist until a person observes it. Jones and Robbins write:

> **The *participatory anthropic principle (PAP)* was proposed by the physicist John Archibald Wheeler when he said that people exist in a "participatory universe." In Wheeler's (extremely controversial) view, an actual observer is needed to cause the collapse of the wavefunction, not just bits and pieces bouncing into each other. ...To John Barrow and Frank Tipler (in their popular and widely controversial 1986 book *The Anthropic Cosmological Principle)*, this means that the universe itself comes into being only if someone is there to observe it. Essentially, the universe requires some form of life present for the wavefunction to collapse in the first place, meaning that the universe itself could not exist without life in it.**[115]

The intelligent-observer paradox seems to indicate that material things are not matter until they are observed with a person's senses. As strange as this sounds, very intelligent scientists have a difficult time finding evidence to the contrary. "Berkley physicist Nick Herbert wryly sums it up: 'One of the best-kept secrets of science is that physicists have lost their grip on reality.'"[116] Is matter really there, or are the stars really in the heavens above the earth, if someone is not looking at them? That leads one to believe people could be living in a three-dimensional digital universe made by God and interpreted by a person's five senses.

Think of God as the grand designer and creator of the physical world. All matter is made up of tiny atoms. Tiny atoms are made up of even more miniature vibrating strings of energy. Essentially everything in the universe is made of tiny vibrating strings of energy that become particles or material when an intelligent observer or a created, eternal being uses their five senses to interpret that which is before them. Atoms are almost entirely empty space. They are not material in whole, nor are they solid. What makes them appear to be solid is the electromagnetic force of the spinning electrons around the nucleus of the atom. This sounds exceptionally far-reaching and impossible, but it confounds the best scientists. With learning more about the molecular structure of matter, science became more philosophical and expanded from laboratory experimentalism. "If matter had no fixed form until observed, if it exists in some insubstantial state until observed, then where does that leave science? As Albert Einstein said, likely speaking for most scientists, 'I like to believe that the moon is there even if I am not looking at it.'"[117]

People may be living in a digitally created universe that is activated by their consciousness. Being a digital universe would speak to the universe's makeup; everything is made up of tiny packages of matter—much like the photon is both wave and a particle or small package of energy, depending on the situation. Missler points out:

> **Still, all matter is found in tiny packages...As we've explored the domain of the exceedingly small, we've discovered that limits exist there as well. Infinity cannot be found in the macrocosm, and it can't be found at the microcosm either. That's the real thing we're going to be bumping up against. At the basis of our physical reality we find indivisible units, and that means our reality is digital. It is a digital simulation, a virtual reality, a shadow of a larger reality that's beyond our comprehension—the metacosm.[118]**

The idea is that people are living in a virtual reality created by a higher being. Life as a person experiences it is like living in a computer game that is three-dimensional. Reporting on a conference of scientists about the possibility of a simulated universe, Clara Moskowitz writes:

> **And there are other reasons to think we might be virtual. For instance, the more we learn about the universe, the more it appears to be based on mathematical laws. Perhaps that is not a given, but a function of the nature of the universe we are living in. "If I were a character in a computer game, I would also discover eventually that the rules seemed completely rigid and mathematical," said Max Tegmark, a cosmologist at the Massachusetts Institute of Technology (MIT). "That just reflects the computer code in which it was written."**[119]

If one interprets atoms as bytes, they can see that the universe is digital. Did God create the universe as a three-dimensional digital world and place people in it with a consciousness and an eternal spirit? This theory is very close to the intelligent-observer theory, but instead of a person's consciousness making everything a reality, everything including a person's physical body is digitally generated. People interpret the data before them with their five virtual senses. The example of a game may not be the best analogy because it seems to insinuate that God is playing a game with this world and mankind. The world is no game, but it may be a three-dimensional simulation that is more real in the spiritual realm than in the so-called "physical" realm. Olivia Solon of *The Guardian* writes an article about the possibility that the world is computer simulated and quotes

Rich Terrile, a scientist at Nasa's Jet Propulsion Laboratory. Solon states:

> **Reasons to believe that the universe is a simulation include the fact that it behaves mathematically and is broken up into pieces (subatomic particles) like a pixelated video game. "Even things that we think of as continuous—time, energy, space, volume—all have a finite limit to their size. If that's the case, then our universe is both computable and finite. Those properties allow the universe to be simulated," Terrile said. "Quite frankly, if we are not living in a simulation, it is an extraordinarily unlikely circumstance," he added.[120]**

The invention of computers is a potential revealing of the creator. The more people discover and create about computers, data, and programming, the more it reveals about a God who has created and programmed the universe as well as people. The more people learn about computers and the computer world, the more they learn about themselves. Computers have hardware and software. Hardware has mass, and software does not.[121] The software is what makes the computer do its computing. The software is the programming, the various functions and processes of the computer. The computer shell or case and parts are the body in which the software resides.

This is much like the human body. There is hardware and software. The hardware is the body and all its parts; it has mass. The software is a person's consciousness, the spirit, the eternal part. The consciousness or spirit has no mass; it cannot be weighed, but it is what gives the hardware life. People attempt to learn about their builder or their beginning by inspecting the elements of their hardware. Just as the finely tuned watch is much less advanced than the watchmaker, humans are much less advanced compared to their maker as well. No indication exists that Neil deGrasse Tyson believes in a higher being. However, he does make a comparison between the intelligence of chimpanzees and humans, and then between the intelligence of humans and the potential higher-dimensional grand programmer:

> **Neil deGrasse Tyson, director of the museum's Hayden Planetarium, put the odds at 50-50 that our entire existence is a program on someone else's hard drive. "I think the likelihood may be very high," he said. He noted the gap between human and chimpanzee intelligence, despite the fact that we share more than 98 percent of our DNA. Somewhere out there could be a being whose intelligence is that much greater than our own. "We would be drooling, blithering idiots in their presence," he said. "If that's the case, it is easy for me to imagine that everything in our lives is just a creation of some other entity for their entertainment."[122]**

It does appear that God created and programmed the universe to be the way it is. The fall of mankind brought sin into the world, changing the rules and adding some laws (Romans 5:12). But God, the grand programmer, was never surprised and had already written the program that would fix the sin virus (Romans 5:8-11).

People have been programmed with eternal software that gives them life. When a person's hardware stops working and dies, their software lives on for an eternity. While people are on the earth, living in the three-dimensional universe, they interpret all the data around them with their five senses. They interpret colors, shapes, materials, everything in the physical three-dimensional world. Living people are stuck in three dimensions and able to perceive only the physical world. However, people are given glimpses of the higher dimension, such as angels coming and going, miracles, the Scriptures (God communicating to mankind from outside of space and time in written form), and various scientific clues pointing to higher dimensions.

Picture a person playing a computerized game on a desktop computer. The person controls certain aspects of the game, while some aspects play themselves out according to the program and the choices made within the program. The person is playing the game, they are involved in the game, but the characters in the game are totally unaware of this person, who they are and where they are. They could be sitting in a room, in a house, or at a table in a coffee shop playing the computer game; the characters have no idea. This is a crude comparison to a person's possible view of their life and the grand programmer who created this three-dimensional world. Dennis Zetting continues the virtual reality model.

> **Take a computer game...in which you assume an avatar identity within the game. From the perspective of that avatar, it is living within the program code laws of the game; that is its reality. It has no understanding that another world exists with completely different laws outside the realm of the game. Nor does the avatar understand what supports its own world. It has no idea of electrical circuits, computer processors and memory chips, let alone non-virtual oxygen, water and fire.** [123]

What if the creator of the virtual reality game left clues of himself in the game for the character to know him? What if the creator of the program communicated to the characters through a written book? What if the creator of the virtual reality program entered the game to provide a way to know the creator and a way of escape from the game? The characters now have access to the creator and can one day exit the game to live in the real world of their creator.

This could explain how higher dimensional beings—angels, for example—appear as three-dimensional beings when they enter the three-dimensional realm. Angels appear as men many times in the Bible. Perhaps a person's consciousness is programmed to interpret the information only when the angels enter their realm. When angels are in the spiritual realm, they remain undetectable to the five senses. A person can interpret only three-dimensional data with their five senses. A person's world is a physical world, but there are clear indicators that there is more to the world than the physical. The deeper a person searches into the quantum world, the more mysterious the world appears to be. Does this quantum weirdness point to a higher dimension or that there is more to the universe than the physical reality? The main lesson from the intelligent-observer paradox may be that there is a spiritual dimension next to a person that is undetectable with their five senses, but there are clues to its existence.

It is also very plausible that when Adam and Eve sinned in the Garden of Eden, they lost the ability to perceive or interpret the spiritual realm or spiritual dimension. This is only speculation because little is known of Adam and Eve before their fall into sin. The fall affected mankind, the animal kingdom, nature, and the universe. There appears to have been a closer relationship with both God and the animal kingdom. Very little is revealed in the Bible about mankind's ability to perceive the spiritual realm before the fall. Once the fall happened, mankind's relationship with God became obstructed because of sin. It is not clear whether sin obstructed the ability to interpret the spiritual realm, or whether God simply removed the ability to perceive and interpret the spiritual realm. Or maybe humans were unable to see the spiritual realm both before and after the fall.

This author leans toward the belief that sin caused humanity to lose its ability to see the spiritual realm clearly and truthfully. After Adam and Eve sinned, they heard God walking to them in the garden. Their relationship with God before they sinned was different after they sinned. Were they able to see God before sinning but not after? Eve was conversing with Satan, a spiritual being, before the fall as if it were normal. The serpent, who spoke to Eve, is Satan. He is either inhabiting a snake's body, or he is called a serpent much like Jesus is called a lamb. This author believes the latter. He is called a serpent because it represents his character. As a result, mankind is left with clues in the three-dimensional realm directing them to a spiritual dimension connected to the consciousness or spirit.

As a result of sin, people can now perceive only with their five senses. When Adam and Eve chose to disobey God and appease their physical desires by taking the fruit and eating it, they were relegated to the three-dimensional physical world man now inhabits. Therefore, they received their desire of being led by their physical senses and lived a life limited to the physical world.

The spiritual world is perceptible to people, but only through the Holy Spirit. A person is born physically into the world as a sinner. Sinners can see only three-dimensionally. ("Jesus answered, 'Most assuredly, I say to you, unless one is born of water and the Spirit, he cannot enter the kingdom of God. That which is born of the flesh is flesh, and that which is born of the Spirit is spirit'" John 3:5-6.) Once someone accepts Jesus Christ as Savior, the spiritual eyes are uncovered, and they can see spiritually—however, they can see only in part. A person will not be able to understand fully in the spiritual realm until they join Christ forever through death or the rapture. 1 Corinthians 13:12 tells us, "For now we see in a mirror, dimly, but then face to face. Now I know in part, but then I shall know just as I also am known."

The computer simulation theory is an interesting way to look at human existence. It brings a whole new angle to the first chapter of Genesis. When God created during the first six days, it is possibly speaking of the turning on of the program that God created. "Let there be light..." could be the initial beginning and release of photons in the universe as the digital atoms are activated. The switch is flipped each day as the universe is created and all that is contained in it comes into existence just as described in the first two chapters of Genesis.

Chapter 7

Incoming Call from: GOD

There is abundant evidence that the Bible, though written by men, is not the product of the human mind. By countless multitudes, it has always been revered as a communication to us from the Creator of the Universe. We must not build on the sands of an uncertain and everchanging science...but upon the rock of inspired Scriptures.

–John Ambrose Fleming (1849-1945), Pioneer of Electronics

Nevertheless, just as I believe that the Book of Scripture illumines the pathway to God, so I believe that the Book of Nature, with its astonishing details—the blade of grass, the Conus cedonulli, or the resonance levels of the carbon atom—also suggests a God of purpose and a God of design. And I think my belief makes me no less a scientist.

–Owen Gingerich, research professor of astronomy and of the history of science emeritus at Harvard University, senior astronomer emeritus at the Smithsonian Astrophysical Observatory

Science points to higher dimensions, and the Bible reveals the reality of higher dimensions. Science also points to a grand designer who created the universe and all that is within it. The grand designer or grand programmer is the one who programmed or created this three-dimensional world in which mankind lives. Has the grand programmer left evidence in His creation of who He is? Are there clues that lead people to who created them? Simply by looking at creation (the universe and living beings), a person can see verification of God. In chapter five, we examined evidence of a Grand Designer. Has the grand programmer communicated directly with His creation? It seems reasonable that the creator of this three-dimensional universe would do so. God, the creator, is outside of mankind's space and time, yet He desires a relationship with His creation. An abundant amount of evidence exists that leads the seeking person to God through merely examining His creation: the universe, the animal kingdom, plants, nature, and mankind.

Did God reveal Himself to mankind through the written word also? If He did, which written word is it? People claim many different religious books are from a higher power, from God, or from a guide from the spiritual dimension. Most religions and spiritual groups have some kind of written word that teaches and guides the group and its followers. It is the position of this author that the Holy Bible is God's communication to people in the three-dimensional world, from outside of space and time where God primarily resides. Why should one believe that the Bible is the Word of God and other writings are not? Tim Burns, a Christian author and speaker, writes:

> **The Christian Bible is a history book and many other history books exist. The Bible comments on a belief system which promises the practitioner peace and a better life. From Confucius to Mohammed, Tony Robbins to L. Ron Hubbard, myriads of books set forth similar claims. So what sets the Bible apart from this mountain of literature?[124]**

While Tim goes on to discuss what sets the Bible apart from other writings that also claim divine direction, the primary reason is that the Bible makes many prophetic claims that come to pass. "One aspect differentiating the Bible from other religious, historical, or inspirational works is this: throughout the Bible, future events are predicted with verifiable accuracy."[125] The prophetic predictions of the future in the Bible are one of the main reasons people regard it as the Word of God. Who else knows the future other than God, the grand programmer of the universe?

The other factor that sets the Bible apart from other spiritual literature is its claim to be from God. The Bible was written over thousands of years by several different and unrelated men. Yet the message is continuous and unified. Many times in the Bible, claims are made of God speaking to people, even though the message was delivered through people. Burns once again states:

> **The writings from the Far East, the teachings of Confucius, Buddhism and Hinduism do not even make a claim to be God's word. They present to their followers a path to a simpler, more satisfactory life. The Muslim Koran makes no claims to being words from Allah. Rather it is the writing of Mohammed, a religious leader, his record of history as well as his desire for the future. But has any prophecy in the Koran come to pass?[126]**

God had a full and close relationship with Adam and Eve before their fall into sin. Humanity's sin became a barrier and separated them from God. People, because of sin, lost their ability to experience the spiritual realm. Mankind's fall into sin caused them to be confined to a three-dimensional world of their five senses, recognizing only the physical realm. God, the grand programmer, desired to restore His relationship with people. Therefore, He reached out to humanity to disclose Himself and make Himself known. He sought to restore the broken relationship and offer eternal, everlasting life. God has revealed Himself to mankind in four specific ways: creation, the written word, Jesus the Messiah, and the Holy Spirit.

Creation

The Bible is clearly written from the perspective that God created the universe, and He is to be worshiped because of who He is and what He has done. God created the universe, earth, and all that is living.

> **By the word of the LORD the heavens were made, and all the host of them by the breath of His mouth. He gathers the waters of the sea together as a heap; He lays up the deep in storehouses. Let all the earth fear the LORD; Let all the inhabitants of the world stand in awe of Him (Psalms 33:6-8).**

> **For by Him all things were created that are in heaven and that are on earth, visible and invisible, whether thrones or dominions or principalities or powers. All things were created through Him and for Him. And He is before all things, and in Him all things consist (Colossians 1:16-17).**

God reveals Himself to humanity in His creation.

> **Because what may be known of God is manifest in them, for God has shown it to them. For since the**

creation of the world His invisible attributes are clearly seen, being understood by the things that are made, even His eternal power and Godhead, so that they are without excuse (Romans 1:19-20).

The Bible declares that worshiping the creation is a result of sin.

Because, although they knew God, they did not glorify Him as God, nor were thankful, but became futile in their thoughts, and their foolish hearts were darkened. Professing to be wise, they became fools, and changed the glory of the incorruptible God into an image made like corruptible man—and birds and four-footed animals and creeping things. Therefore God also gave them up to uncleanness, in the lusts of their hearts, to dishonor their bodies among themselves, who exchanged the truth of God for the lie, and worshiped and served the creature rather than the Creator, who is blessed forever (Romans 1:21-25).

The Bible exhorts people to worship the creator.

You alone are the LORD; You have made heaven, the heaven of heavens, with all their host, the earth and everything on it, the seas and all that is in them, and You preserve them all. The host of heaven worships You (Nehemiah 9:6).

You are worthy, O Lord, to receive glory and honor and power; for You created all things, and by Your will they exist and were created (Revelation 4:11).

The Written Word

As a result of mankind's sin and the broken relationship, God seeks to make Himself known to people. The Holy Bible is a record of God speaking with people to communicate the plan of salvation through the promise of a Messiah. Much of the Bible is a historical narrative that is from God to mankind, though written through people. Some of the Bible is commandments to follow directed at specific people groups. But all of the Bible is inspired by the Holy Spirit for learning and application. How can one trust the Bible as inspired truth from the God and creator of all things? Those who research and seek with an open mind whether the Bible is from God will find the answer to be that it most certainly is—for it is prophetically, scientifically, and historically accurate.

If the creator and grand programmer wanted to get a written message to His creation, how would He do it? First of all, He would want to make certain it was not confused with imitations. He would make it stand out supernaturally, by using prophecy. Only God exists outside of space and time and knows the whole of time, past and future. Only God knows the future and what will happen. God can validate His message by integrating prophetic insights throughout the document. Additionally, God can integrate His message throughout His Word so that it cannot be lost or confused. God would have a central message that would be built upon and repeated in various ways without contradictions. Missler says that God does have a way of authenticating His message throughout the entire collection of books called the Bible. He asserts:

> **[God] tells us in advance, from ancient times, things that are not yet done. He demonstrates His ability to be outside of time itself by giving us the future before it happens—centuries in advance. We see it over**

> **and over throughout the Bible. These 66 books are written out by at least 40 authors, yet together they give us a single story, an integrated message from outside our time domain.**[127]

Several areas of objective evidence lead one to believe that the Bible is true and a supernatural book that God has used to communicate with people. Five areas will be examined that lend credibility to and provide sufficient evidence for believing the Bible is a supernatural book communicated from outside of man's space and time: archaeology, manuscript evidence, early Church writings, an integrated message, and—the greatest evidence of all—prophecy. While examining each area is impressive, adding them together provides more than sufficient reason to believe the Bible is from God.

1. **Archaeology.** The Bible is a historical record of people and places going back thousands of years. Hundreds of archeological finds substantiate the statements in the Bible. Archaeology is one of the ways people know they can trust the Bible as historically reliable. Ralph Muncaster is the Executive Director of the Institute of Contemporary Christian Faith and author of the book *A Skeptic's Search for God, Dismantling Evolution*. He makes the point that archaeology gives credibility to the Bible. Archaeology confirms the stories and events are not fantasy. Muncaster writes:

> **When the [archaeological] evidence is used together with other evidence of communication from God in the Bible (for example, prophecy, scientific insights, concealed evidence), it helps confirm that God exists, that God communicates, and that the biblical message is a real message to us.**[128]

Numerous archeological discoveries confirm the location of cities, people, rulers, and events recorded in the Bible. Muncaster continues, "There is far more historical evidence for the Bible than for any other ancient document ever written."[129]

Many scholars accept evolution as fact and then look to substantiate their beliefs with evidence from archaeology. Once Darwin's theory of humans evolving from lower animal life forms was embraced by scientists as fact, paleontologists searched for fossilized evidence of evolution. The search was on to find the missing links, to uncover the thousands of "in-between" life forms that were assumed to be fossilized in various parts of the world. However, paleontologists have been disappointed that no such treasure trove of "prehistorical" fossilized humans has been located. Some of the so-called "prehistoric humans" that were found proved to be false and even deliberate frauds.[130] "Many such 'tractional forms' eventually proved to be animals, not human. Examples are Colorado man (a horse), Ramapithecus (an extinct ape), Nebraska Man (an extinct pig), and 'Lucy'—an ape."[131] The remaining few possible prehistoric human finds are highly debatable due to their condition and the date they lived on the earth.

Instead, archeological discoveries proved that people were highly intelligent thousands of years ago. Instead of finding evidence of cavemen learning how to use basic tools, it was discovered that people were building amazing architectural structures. Evolution teaches that people grew intellectually from a monkey to a human, but the Bible teaches that people were created with intelligence. Adam and Eve were created perfectly before the fall and with full brain capacity. If that is the case, then archaeology cannot help but reveal mankind's intelligence. Ken Ham, CEO and founder of Answers in Genesis and world-renowned author and speaker, writes:

> **From an evolutionary perspective, most people today believe that ancient man originally communicated with grunts, eventually developed language, and then over time went from making "primitive" items (e.g., stone tools) to working with bronze and iron. But the evidence Don [Landis] and his researchers have collected from around the globe refutes this false evolutionary view of human history.**[132]

As an example, the archeological excavations of the city of Ur reveal a much more advanced civilization than scholars presumed would be found at that time. The mathematical tablets recovered from Ur showed that civilization during the time when Abraham lived was more intelligent than once believed. The tablets showed that knowledge of the Pythagorean Theorem already existed. Dr. Clifford Wilson was a well-respected archeologist, devout Christian, and creationist who held a Ph.D. from the University of South Carolina. Wilson stated, "In the modern version of this theorem we are told that in a right-handed triangle the square on the hypotenuse equals the sum of the squares on the other two sides. That theorem is not stated as such on this tablet, but its text showed that the principle was known. It was used in building construction."[133]

The construction method of the houses unearthed in Ur also gave affirmation that the people were much more advanced in building than once thought. The houses were found to have septic systems that carried human waste away from the houses for sanitation purposes. "Some houses even had a system of clay pipes fitted so that the refuse could flow from the house."[134]

The large size of the city of Ur surprised many scholars, who mistakenly assumed that cities were not that large two thousand years before Christ. Andrew Lawler for *National Geographic* writes about the discoveries at Ur:

> **But the real heyday came around 2000 B.C., when Ur dominated southern Mesopotamia after the fall of the Akkadian Empire. The sprawling city was home to more than 60,000 people, and included quarters for foreigners as well as large factories producing wool clothes and carpets exported abroad. Traders from India and the Persian Gulf crowded the busy wharves, and caravans arrived regularly from what is now northern Iraq and Turkey.**[135]

Other archaeological discoveries that help bolster the reliability of the Bible are listed below:

The Enuma Elish is the Babylonian account of creation, while the Epic of Gilgamesh is the account of a Babylonian flood. These discoveries support the first chapters of Genesis being the truth. Though accounts of the nations are corrupted and fanciful, they give witness that the truth was there at one time.[136]

The city of Nineveh – "The history of Nineveh, the capital of the Assyrian Empire, was regarded as a Biblical myth by scholars who denied even the existence of this ancient city until 1849 when the ruins were discovered, validating the Biblical accounts."[137]

The Babylonian empire – Babylonian bricks have been recovered from the time of Nebuchadnezzar, revealing his boastfulness as a king.[138] Thousands of Babylonian ruins and artifacts have been unearthed, giving validity to the truth of all the biblical accounts of Babylon's existence. The greatest of these artifacts is believed to be the Nabonidus Chronicle, which records that Daniel was the third ruler in the Babylonian kingdom.[139]

The biblical account of the Hittites – The Hittites mentioned many times in the Old Testament were for years believed by secular scholars to be an imaginary civilization dreamt up by biblical writers. Then, some archaeological discoveries in 1876–1880 were being attributed to the Hittites from the Bible. Opponents seized upon the claim as ridiculous. David Down was a field archaeologist in the Middle East who, for nearly twenty years, published a monthly archaeology magazine called, *Archaeology Diggings*. Down wrote several books on archaeology and recorded a weekly radio talk on archaeology for many years. He writes about those discoveries, "The critics went off into peals of laughter. Why, everyone knew that the Hittites were just a figment of biblical imagination, or at best, some insignificant tribe occupying a corner of Palestine at the time of the Israelite invasion."[140] It took a few years of study and analysis, but the Bible was once again confirmed by archaeology. Down continues:

> **Finally in 1884, William Wright published a book, *The Empire of the Hittites*, in which he presented such a mass of scholarly evidence that there could**

> **be no further resistance and the critics had to hide their faces. The Hittites had not only been positively identified, but had taken their place as one of the great nations of antiquity.**[141]

Many more archeological discoveries exist that help substantiate the accuracy of the historical elements of the Bible, thus giving it a firm foundation for additional evidence substantiating it as a word from the grand programmer, God. Many of the pieces of the archaeological evidence are small and somewhat insignificant by themselves, but they point to a very reliable piece of communication when taken as a group. Paul E. Little worked for twenty-five years with InterVarsity Christian Fellowship. He was also a professor at Trinity Evangelical Divinity School and the author of several books. He says, "More than 25,000 sites showing some connection with the Old Testament period have been located in Bible lands."[142] Very few archaeological discoveries have an apparent contradiction with the Bible. Nearly always, the archaeological discovery supports and verifies the biblical account.[143]

2. Manuscript Evidence. Some of the greatest evidence for the accuracy of Scripture is the sheer number of biblical texts found in the world. The New Testament writings were immediately recognized as special and divine when they were written. Copies were made and passed to churches so they could also benefit from the sacred writings that were being called Scripture. Even the New Testament writers recognized the writings as inspired Scripture. Both Jesus and Peter use the word "Scriptures" to describe the divine writings. "Jesus answered and said to them, 'Are you not therefore mistaken, because you do not know the Scriptures nor the power of God?'" (Mark 12:24). "For prophecy never came by the will of man, but holy men of God spoke as they were moved by the Holy Spirit" (2 Peter 1:21).

Sean McDowell, the son of Josh McDowell who wrote the book *Evidence that Demands a Verdict,* comments on the number of New Testament manuscripts that have been found as of 2017. Sean and his father co-author the newly updated book called *Evidence.* In an article from Sean's website, he writes:

> **It is extremely laborious to track down the number of both classical and biblical manuscripts. We had a team of researchers and scholars help us with this endeavor. Still, for a variety of reasons, these numbers are educated guesses. We list the numbers for other classical works and specific biblical manuscripts in the updated *Evidence*. But here are the key manuscript updates:**
> **Greek Manuscript total: 5,856**
> **Earliest manuscript: AD 130 (John Rylands Papyrus: P52)**
> **Non-Greek Manuscripts (Armenian, Latin, etc.): 18,130+**
>
> **Total Manuscripts: 23,986**[144]

The Old Testament manuscripts and writings are very impressive. The Dead Sea Scrolls were discovered in eleven caves along the northwest shore of the Dead Sea between the years 1947 and 1956. Fragments of every book of the Hebrew Bible or Old Testament, except for the book of Esther, were found.[145] The significance of the Dead Sea Scrolls is immense for biblical scholars. They answer the question of how someone can know the Bible today has been passed down truthfully and has a reliable message. Until these texts became available, the oldest Hebrew Old Testament text in existence dated back to AD 800. No original manuscripts of the Bible exist today, so the next best thing is to go back to the oldest copies that would be closest to the originals. The Dead Sea Scrolls are eight hundred to a thousand years older than previously known manuscripts, dating to around 200 BC. What the Dead Sea Scroll manuscripts clearly demonstrate is that during a span of approximately a thousand years there was essentially no significant alteration in the text. The scribes who transcribed the text of the Bible were very detailed. They had high standards of accuracy, counting every word to make sure it was an exact copy. Josh McDowell writes:

> **When finally finished, the scribe's manuscript had to be certified as having been transcribed correctly. Some traditions required three separate rabbis to check the accuracy! This meant these persons had to completely unroll this 72-foot scroll to check and count every single word and all 304,805 of the letters. They had to be sure there was the same number of letters in this scroll compared to the Torah from which it was copied.**[146]

Their attention to detail was suspected by many scholars, but the Dead Sea Scrolls were an archaeological confirmation that this was precisely the case. The Old Testament writings were clearly held as divine by the Jewish Rabbis and people as soon as the writings were done. Manuscript evidence shows that the writings are neither fabricated nor riddled with errors.

The evidence also points to a grand designer who desires to communicate with people.

3. **Early Church Fathers' Writings.** The New Testament writings were initially written between AD 35 to AD 100. The biblical authors claimed firsthand, eyewitness accounts, just as Luke does at the beginning of his gospel account.

> **Inasmuch as many have taken in hand to set in order a narrative of those things which have been fulfilled among us, just as those who from the beginning were eyewitnesses and ministers of the word delivered them to us, it seemed good to me also, having had perfect understanding of all things from the very first, to write to you an orderly account, most excellent Theophilus (Luke 1:1-3).**

Peter also claims his writing was an eyewitness account. "For we did not follow cunningly devised fables when we made known to you the power and coming of our Lord Jesus Christ, but were eyewitnesses of His majesty" (2 Peter 1:16). John claims to be an eyewitness in two different writings. "And he who has seen has testified, and his testimony is true; and he knows that he is telling the truth, so that you may believe" (John 19:35). "That which we have seen and heard we declare to you, that you also may have fellowship with us; and truly our fellowship is with the Father and with His Son Jesus Christ" (1 John 1:3). The New Testament writings were written by eyewitnesses and are truthful regarding what happened during the life of Jesus and the first years of the church. The originals were copied by churches to be read in their services and studied by followers of Christ.

For the next one hundred to two hundred years after the originals were written, many church fathers commented on what has now become known as the New Testament writings. Ron Rhodes holds a Th.D. from Dallas Theological Seminary; he is the president of Reasoning from the Scriptures Ministries and has authored over sixty books. Rhodes writes:

> **...there are over 86,000 quotations of the New Testament in the early church fathers. There are also New Testament quotations in thousands of early church Lectionaries (worship books). There are enough quotations from the early church fathers that even if we did not have a single copy of the Bible, scholars could still reconstruct all but 11 verses of the entire New Testament from material written within 150 to 200 years from the time of Christ.**[147]

These extra-biblical writings are beneficial in determining when the New Testament writings were originally written. When someone is commenting on a New Testament book in the first or second century, then the book must have already been written. The early church fathers' writings also help scholars to determine any textual variants and translation issues. If certain passages were quoted fifty years after the original was written, there is a good chance the quote will be the best reading of the text. Patrick Zukeran has received graduate degrees from Dallas Theological Seminary and Southern Evangelical Seminary and has written several books. He writes:

> **Clement of Rome, whose writings date to 95 AD, quotes from three of the gospels and other portions of the New Testament. Ignatius, Bishop of Antioch, writes a letter before his martyrdom in Rome in 115**

AD quoting from the four gospels and other New Testament letters. Polycarp wrote to the Philippians in 120 AD and specifically mentions the gospels and New Testament letters. Justin Martyr (150 AD) cites John 3. Several church fathers from the first century are familiar with New Testament works, especially the gospels, and refer to them as inspired Scripture. From these writings we can conclude that the gospels were written and in circulation by the end of the first century AD.[148]

The tremendous manuscript evidence helps people accept the Bible as a truthful, trustworthy book.

4. **Integrated Message.** Over forty authors were writing at different times over a span of thousands of years. The Bible delivers the message of salvation and grace throughout its various books written by authors from different time periods, most of whom never knew each other. God has skillfully woven His message throughout the Bible so it could not be corrupted, removed, or imitated. Concerning the consistent message of the Bible, Missler writes:

Over the course of my life, I've discovered that these 66 books we call the Bible, accumulated over the course of 2,000 years by more than 40 different writers are an integrated message system from One Author. I spent 30 years in the strategic arena, but my technical background is in the information sciences. I'm using these terms precisely. These 66 books were written over thousands of years, and yet the great discovery to make is that every detail has been placed in those pages deliberately, anticipated by skillful design. They are not 66 individual books, but one entire package from beginning to end.[149]

The message of the Bible is timeless. It is as easily understood in the year 2000 AD as it was in 2000 BC. Consistent symbols are found in the Bible throughout the Old and New Testaments. For example, light and darkness are commonly understood word pictures for good and evil even today. The Bible is consistent in using the light and dark analogies throughout its pages.

5. **Prophecy.** The Bible contains multiple prophecies that are predicted and come to pass just as they were written. This is, without a doubt, the most significant evidence that the Bible is of supernatural origin. Some prophecies were so clearly predicted and fulfilled that many skeptics have claimed the prophecies were written after the fact. Many of the writers knew they were speaking on behalf of God. Little, confirming this, writes, "'The word of the LORD came to me' is a phrase that recurs frequently in the Old Testament. David says, 'The Spirit of the LORD spoke through me; his word was on my tongue' (2 Samuel 23:2). Jeremiah said, 'The LORD reached out his hand and touched my mouth and said to me, 'Now, I have put my words in your mouth'" (Jeremiah 1:9).[150]

Daniel's prophecies must be the most amazing and detailed prophecies in the Bible. His prophecies concerning the coming kingdoms, especially Greece and the Romans, are a validation that God was speaking through him. Daniel gives the 490-year timeline for the Jewish people. He also predicts some very specific events that occur after the fall of Greece about Antiochus Epiphanes that are so specific, critics claim it was written after the events took place. Walvoord writes, "For so striking was the reliability of what the prophet foretold, that he could not appear to unbelievers as a predictor of the future, but rather a narrator of things already past."[151] Dan Hayden of Dallas Theological Seminary comments on the importance of Daniel's prophecies:

> **Daniel describes the exact ebb and flow of four empires from Babylon to Medo-Persia to Greece to Rome. He even foresaw the meteoric rise to power of the Greek conqueror Alexander the Great, as well as the final division of his Greek empire by four of his surviving generals (Daniel 7:6, 8:5–8, 11:2–4). Desperate to counter the implications of this prophetic phenomenon, nineteenth-century skeptics concocted dating schemes that placed the time of Daniel's writing after the events. Careful research by modern textual scholars, however, has validated the early origin of this prophecy, establishing Daniel as the authentic author. Daniel's prophecy is a genuine "wow," which clearly gives evidence of the Bible's divine nature.[152]**

The book of Daniel is a point of attack for all Bible critics because of its specific and bold prophecies. The Dead Sea Scrolls were a major victory for Daniel supporters as the dating of the oldest manuscripts immediately went from 800 AD to 150 BC. This placed the writing so close to the period between the Old and New Testaments that the time for a pseudo-Daniel writer was now extremely limited and highly unlikely. Liberal scholars claimed that the prophecies of Daniel were written well after the time of Daniel by an author or authors other than Daniel himself. The discovery of Daniel fragments and scrolls, as part of the Dead Sea Scroll finds, eliminated that argument. It was clear that the book of Daniel had already been accepted as an inspired prophetic writing by 150 BC.

Many prophecies were written about the coming of Christ and His ministry. God chose to write to people about the coming Messiah, so they would recognize Him and not be led astray by imitations. Chuck Missler lists several prophecies in the Old Testament about Jesus Christ.

Of the line of David (2 Samuel 7:12-16; Psalm 89:3-4, 110:1, 132:11; Isaiah 9:6, 7, 11:1)
Born of a virgin (Genesis 3:15; Isaiah 7:14)
Born in Bethlehem (Micah 5:2)
A sojourner in Egypt (Hosea 11:1)
A Galilean (Isaiah 9:1, 2), and in Nazareth (Isaiah 11:1)
Announced by an Elijah-like herald (Isaiah 40:3-5; Malachi 3:1, 4:5)
An occasion for the slaughter of Bethlehem's children (Genesis 35:19-20; Jeremiah 31:15)
Bringing liberty to the captives (Isaiah 58:6, 61:1)
A hero to the Gentiles (Isaiah 42:1-4)
A substitute for our griefs and punishment (Isaiah 53:4-5)
A healer (Isaiah 53:4-5)
A teacher of parables (Isaiah 6:9-10; Psalm 78:2)
Disbelieved, rejected (Psalm 69:4, 118:22; Isaiah 6:10, 29:13, 53:1)
A humble King entering Jerusalem (Zechariah 9:9; Psalm 118:26)
Betrayed by a friend (Psalm 41:9)
Betrayed for 30 pieces of silver (Zechariah 11:1-13)
Like a smitten shepherd (Zechariah 13:7)
Given vinegar and gall (Psalm 69:21)
Pierced (Zechariah 12:10; Psalm 22:16)
Bones unbroken (like the Passover lamb) (Exodus 12:46; Numbers 9:12; Psalm 34:20)
Killed along with malefactors (Isaiah 53:9, 12)
Buried in a rich man's grave (Isaiah 53:9)
Raised from the dead on the 3rd day (Genesis 22:4;

Psalm 16:10-11; Jonah 1:7; Hosea 6:2) Resurrected, followed by the destruction of Jerusalem (Daniel 9:26, 11:31, 12:1, 11).[153]

Missler discusses a few of the prophecies that would be very difficult to fulfill; he lays out the probability for the prophecies to be fulfilled by a single person. He posits that the odds one person could fulfill even eight of these predictions are extremely low. "We have the probability of each individual one, and a large number of people might have fulfilled one or two of these. What's the composite probability of all of them?"[154] Missler gives a visual example of how remote the chances are. He explains that it would be comparable to filling the state of Texas two feet high with silver dollars and marking only one of the silver dollars with paint, then asking a person to choose one silver dollar from all those available from Houston to Denton, and from El Paso to Longview. The chance that the person would pick the silver dollar with the special marking is the same as Jesus fulfilling only eight of the Old Testament prophecies.[155]

Jesus the Messiah

Jesus was God in the flesh. He came to earth to offer salvation to people. Jesus' life, death, and resurrection are evidence for the grand programmer, God. Jesus performed hundreds of miracles during His three years of ministry in Israel. He did the miracles not just to help people and heal the sick. He was proving that He was God in the flesh. That is a hard sell. If a person claims to be God, most people will think he is crazy. Jesus did miracle after miracle to prove He had power over the curse of sin. He had power over the curse on nature, over the curse on mankind, and over the curse of death. Jesus' claim to be God was a huge claim, but He backed it up repeatedly. His resurrection from the dead was His final proof that He is God eternal. God, the grand programmer, entered His program and became a character, Jesus Christ. He was born into the program and lived among His creation.

Jesus performed miracles, fulfilled prophecies, and rose from the dead. All of these together point to a God who not only created this universe but came to earth as a man to allow people to restore their relationship with God and live forever.

> **"In the beginning was the Word, and the Word was with God, and the Word was God" (John 1:1).**

> **"No one has seen God at any time. The only begotten Son, who is in the bosom of the Father, He has declared Him" (John 1:18).**

> **"'Behold, the virgin shall be with child, and bear a Son, and they shall call His name 'Immanuel,' which is translated, 'God with us'" (Matthew 1:23).**

Adam and Eve were created perfect and without sin in the beginning. They lived in the Garden of Eden and had one rule—to not eat from the Tree of Knowledge of Good and Evil. Adam and Eve's sin broke the relationship they had with God and left them separated spiritually and physically. Their life of independence from God was tragic and left them broken. Adam and Eve tried to cover their shame with fig leaves. This is a picture of people attempting to cover their sin in their own power and through works. God desired to re-establish His relationship with Adam and Eve, so He stepped in and clothed Adam and Eve with clothes of animal skins. This is a picture of God covering a person's shame and sin through the death and sacrifice of another life, an animal. The first death in the Bible took place in Genesis 3:21: "Also for Adam and his wife the Lord God made tunics of skin, and clothed them." In the making of the clothes, an animal was sacrificed. This is a picture and foreshadowing of the death and sacrifice of Jesus Christ on the cross for humanity's sin.

Holy Spirit

God uses the Holy Spirit to communicate with people. God Himself transcends the spiritual realm and the three-dimensional realm through the Holy Spirit. To unbelievers, "the Holy Spirit bears witness to the truth regarding Jesus Christ."[156] The Holy Spirit also convicts unbelievers of their sin and need for salvation. Torrey writes, the Holy Spirit "convicts (that is, convinces with a convincing that is self-condemning) the world of its sin in not believing on Christ."[157] The Holy Spirit is an immaterial being who is God, along with God the Father and God the Son. Explaining how the conviction of the unbeliever by the Holy Spirit is accomplished, Ryrie states, "Most likely there are several ways involved. The Spirit may speak directly to a person's conscience, which, though able to be seared, can still convict. He may speak through the written Word. He may also use the spoken testimony or preached word."[158] The Bible says:

> **Nevertheless I tell you the truth. It is to your advantage that I go away; for if I do not go away, the Helper will not come to you; but if I depart, I will send Him to you. And when He has come, He will convict the world of sin, and of righteousness, and of judgment: of sin, because they do not believe in Me; of righteousness, because I go to My Father and you see Me no more; of judgment, because the ruler of this world is judged (John 16:7-11).**

The Bible clearly states that the Helper, the Holy Spirit, will convict unbelievers of their sin.

The Holy Spirit indwells the believer when he accepts Jesus Christ as God and Savior. The believer is a living temple where God the Holy Spirit dwells: "Do you not know that your body is the temple of the Holy Spirit" (1 Corinthians 6:19). The Holy Spirit also communicates with the believer. The Bible teaches us about several aspects of the Holy Spirit that are considered communication from the spiritual realm to a person's three-dimensional world.

The Holy Spirit strengthens a person's inward spirit. From the spiritual realm, the Holy Spirit strengthens a person's spirit in growth, times of difficulties, and in the daily Christian walk. "That He would grant you, according to the riches of His glory, to be strengthened with might through His Spirit in the inner man" (Ephesians 3:16).

The Holy Spirit confirms to a person's spirit that he is a believer, a child of God. "The Spirit Himself bears witness with our spirit that we are children of God" (Romans 8:16).

The Holy Spirit guides the believer in knowing what is true and what is false. The Holy Spirit gives the believer discernment from the spiritual realm. "However, when He, the Spirit of truth, has come, He will guide you into all truth; for He will not speak on His own authority, but whatever He hears He will speak; and He will tell you things to come" (John 16:13).

The Holy Spirit calls a believer to surrender, to serve the Lord, and to full-time Christian service.

> **As they ministered to the Lord and fasted, the Holy Spirit said, "Now separate to Me Barnabas and Saul for the work to which I have called them." Then, having fasted and prayed, and laid hands on them, they sent them away (Acts 13:2-4).**

The Holy Spirit gives daily guidance. The Holy Spirit leads the believer in where to go and where not to go.

> **Now when they had gone through Phrygia and the region of Galatia, they were forbidden by the Holy Spirit to preach the word in Asia. After they had come to Mysia, they tried to go into Bithynia, but the Spirit did not permit them. So passing by Mysia, they came down to Troas. And a vision appeared to Paul in the night. A man of Macedonia stood and pleaded with him, saying, "Come over to Macedonia and help us" (Acts 16:6-9).**

Clearly, God uses the Holy Spirit to communicate with people. That communication was certainly disrupted and hindered by sin and the fall. As a result, people today must listen to the Holy Spirit on purpose in their life. While navigating through this three-dimensional world of good and evil, believers must actively listen for the communication of God through the Holy Spirit from the spiritual realm.

God has revealed Himself to people through creation, the written word, coming in person to live among His creation, and through the Holy Spirit. The written word points a person to his creator, God. The evidence shows that God has communicated with mankind through the Bible. The Bible is a supernatural book that explains why people are the way they are, why the world is the way it is, and why Jesus came to do what He did. The Holy Spirit leads the unbeliever to God and guides believers as they follow God in the three-dimensional world.

Chapter 8

Here, There, and Everywhere: The Multidimensionality of God

Finite man cannot comprehend an omnipresent, omniscient, omnipotent, and infinite God. Any effort to visualize God, to reduce him to our comprehension, to describe him in our language, beggars his greatness.

–*Wernher Von Braun (1912-1977), rocket engineer, founder of Astronautics*

As the depth of our insight into the wonderful works of God increases, the stronger are our feelings of awe and veneration in contemplating them and in endeavoring to approach their Author...So will he [the earnest student] by his studies and successive acquirements be led through nature up to nature's God.

–*William Lord Kelvin (d. 1907), inventor of the Kelvin temperature scale*

God is the grand programmer, designer, and creator of the universe. God communicated and still communicates with people through the Holy Bible. The Bible reveals how God relates to people and how people are to relate to God. Life in this three-dimensional world is man's only experience to draw upon when thinking of God. As a result, people tend to visualize God in a three-dimensional way. Though the Bible gives a glimpse into God and the spiritual realm, its illustrations and analogies are three-dimensional. Many times, God is spoken of as having human parts. This is a way to relay a complex message of what God is doing or who He is to a simple, three-dimensional person. Parents do this when trying to explain complex concepts to their children. They must break it down into terminology and words that children can comprehend.

In the Bible, God is described with human parts or doing something as a human would do it. The term used for this is anthropomorphism. The *Holman Bible Dictionary* explains what this is:

> **It [anthropomorphism] is the process of applying human characteristics to a god, an animal, or an inanimate object. The English word is derived from combining two Greek words—*anthropos,* which means *man or mankind,* and *morphe,* which means *form or shape.* Thus, anthropomorphism is giving human form to something not inherently human. In biblical studies the term focuses on those human characteristics applied to God.**[159]

Several verses demonstrate this:

"The LORD make His face shine upon you, and be gracious to you" (Numbers 6:25).

"And the Egyptians shall know that I am the LORD, when I stretch out My hand on Egypt and bring out the children of Israel from among them" (Exodus 7:5).

"The eyes of the LORD are on the righteous, and His ears are open to their cry" (Psalm 34:15).

"Incline Your ear, O LORD, and hear; open Your eyes, O LORD, and see; and hear the words of Sennacherib, which he has sent to reproach the living God" (2 Kings 19:16).

Thinking about God with a three-dimensional mind can lead to seeing God as a superhero like Superman or even as someone like Santa Claus who will give people whatever they want when they ask. When describing God theologically, one would list God's attributes. The Bible describes God's character and the divine qualities or properties that make Him God. Many times, this is done through seeing how He relates with people, and other times it is merely stated. When He spoke to the woman at the well, Jesus told her that God is spirit. "God is Spirit, and those who worship Him must worship in spirit and truth" (John 4:24).

Other times a story reveals an attribute or attributes. In Exodus, when Moses is asking Pharaoh to let the Israelites go, the plagues and the crossing of the Red Sea are examples of God's power or omnipotence. God's attributes are not only descriptions of what He can do, but also of who He is. They are the qualities that make Him who He is. Thinking of God's qualities in only three dimensions can lead to an attempt to make God a very powerful super-human or a mythological god. Thinking of God's attributes from a multidimensional point of view helps one understand the vastness and greatness of God. Even though human beings cannot totally understand higher dimensions, it is crucial to see God as not only greater than His creation, but also outside of His creation's dimensional space and time. Let's examine several of God's primary attributes or characteristics from a multidimensional point of view.

God Is Light

Though God being light is not listed as an attribute in any of the theological books, it is important to consider it from a scientific aspect. The Bible declares that God is light. "This is the message which we have heard from Him and declare to you, that God is light and in Him is no darkness at all" (1 John 1:5). Throughout the Bible, God is analogous to light, and darkness is analogous to evil. Most people understand this comparison, and it is a theme even in the world as a result of its biblical foundation. *Star Wars*, the movie, is a prime example of light versus darkness, which is good versus evil. The fact that God is light is much deeper than an analogy. God being light is fundamental in science, and it permeates the very core of the universe.

"The Bible is also transcendent of parallax, just like light. Light has no parallax. What does that mean? Parallax is an optical term that indicates that something has its focus set. The Bible applied to the people in David's time, and it still applies to us today, because God doesn't change who He is," writes Missler.[160] Comparing the consistency of light with the consistency of God, he continues, "It's interesting that the attributes of God have their parallel in light itself. God is located at infinity. Light has no parallax; its focus is at infinity. God is omnipresent and omniscient. Light particles—photons—communicate instantly, faster than light can travel."[161] The more we learn about light and its properties, God being light brings a new perspective to the analogy. Light has been studied for thousands of years, and scientists have learned much about light and its properties. Light is sometimes matter and sometimes energy. Light behaves strangely when observed. Light is a wave and a particle. However, despite how much scientists have learned, many aspects of light—such as wave-particle duality—are still a mystery.

Most people think of light as what a person can see. This is visible light. Scientists, when they speak of light, sometimes refer to the full spectrum of light. "The spectrum is comprised of different wave types: radio waves, x-ray waves and gamma waves. All of these waves are types of light, yet only visible light allows us to see objects."[162] Therefore, visible light is only a fraction of the spectrum of light. Light is everywhere, as God is everywhere. The waves that make up the spectrum of light are everywhere in the universe. They are in empty space, the ocean, man, animals—light waves are everywhere. Light is what makes the electromagnetic force possible. Light is the force that helps atoms stick together. Electromagnetism is a form of light and binds atoms to other atoms.[163] Zetting discusses the importance of light:

> **If it weren't for electromagnetism, there would not be much of anything preventing one hand from going through the other, or someone walking through a wall. But then again, without electromagnetism, the atoms could not bond in the first place, so there would be no brick wall. Every substance around us is held together by light. If it weren't for light, there would be no stars, planets, people, books, ink, gnats, or politicians...nothing. Light is the universal glue. The universe would not exist without it.[164]**

God is light, but at the same time, He has character, personality, emotions, and attributes. God being light is the foundation for all the attributes that make up who He is. God is outside of mankind's three dimensions of space, and yet He permeates through all the three-dimensional world just as light does. God is invisible, yet He allows glimpses of Himself on a small scale through creation, the written Word, and Jesus Christ. Selbie writes:

> **The fact is that we are mostly insensible to the world around us. It is safe to say that our senses simply cannot detect more than 99.9 percent of the wavelengths, frequencies, and vibrating substances that are actually present. If we could perceive reality fully, the picture we would have in our minds-eye would be almost completely different from the picture our senses allow us to perceive.**[165]

God is much the same. Just as man detects less than 0.1% of the wavelengths, frequencies, and vibrating substances that are present, man perceives only a small portion of who and what God really is. Therefore, the Bible is so important to people because the Word is God communicating who He is and how His relationship with mankind can be re-established in language people can understand with their three-dimensional minds.

Another comparison of God with light is that light is a constant. Light moves at 186,000 miles per second, and it is not impacted by space or time. God is eternal and never changing. He is not affected by space or time. "For I am the LORD, I do not change; Therefore you are not consumed, O sons of Jacob"

(Malachi 3:6). "Have you not known? Have you not heard? The everlasting God, the LORD, the Creator of the ends of the earth, neither faints nor is weary. His understanding is unsearchable" (Isaiah 40:28).

Jesus, being God, claimed to be the light of the world. There is undoubtedly a message and illustration in the analogy. Knowing the properties of light and the character of God, the analogy has a new and deeper meaning. "Then Jesus spoke to them again, saying, 'I am the light of the world. He who follows Me shall not walk in darkness, but have the light of life'" (John 8:12). "To open their eyes, in order to turn them from darkness to light, and from the power of Satan to God, that they may receive forgiveness of sins and an inheritance among those who are sanctified by faith in Me" (Acts 26:18). "For it is the God who commanded light to shine out of darkness, who has shone in our hearts to give the light of the knowledge of the glory of God in the face of Jesus Christ" (2 Corinthians 4:6).

Multidimensionality of God as Spirit

God is spirit, the Bible declares. "God is Spirit, and those who worship Him must worship in spirit and truth" (John 4:24). Understanding God as a spirit is more easily done when we realize that He is outside of man's space and time. Being a spirit does not necessarily mean that He cannot manifest Himself materially in mankind's three-dimensional world. The Bible says that angels are spirit beings. "And of the angels He says: 'Who makes His angels spirits and His ministers a flame of fire'" (Hebrews 1:7). Many times, angels appear as shining men or as human men. Though angels are spiritual beings, they can also have a body in the three-dimensional world. God, too, can appear in a material form in the three-dimensional world. He appeared as a cloud by day and fire by night to the Israelites fleeing Egypt. He appeared as fire in a burning bush to Moses, and He appeared as the Angel of Jehovah to several people in the Old Testament.

Returning to chapter two where Flatman can perceive only two dimensions, he could in no way see a three-dimensional object. Flatman could see only what touched his two-dimensional world. People can see of God only what intersects their world. God is an invisible spirit that can be visible to people at times. Theologian and Bible expositor R.A Torrey says that God is a spirit who has manifested Himself in visible form in times past. He makes two propositions: "First proposition: What was seen in these manifestations of God was not God himself—God in his invisible essence—but a manifestation of God."[166] An apparent contradiction to a person seeing God exists in at least two passages, Exodus 24:9-10 and Isaiah 6:1. Torrey suggests that the apparent contradiction can be easily solved by understanding that these people saw not God, but a manifestation of Him. Torrey illustrates using the comparison of seeing someone's reflection in a mirror. The person was never actually seen; only his reflection was seen.[167] The same would be true of seeing a photograph of someone or seeing a person on television. The person's image was seen, but not the actual person.

A second proposition is made by Torrey. "The angel of the Lord is clearly identified with Jehovah—a visible manifestation of Jehovah."[168] Torrey, along with many other literal biblical scholars, accepts that the Angel of the Lord or the Angel of Jehovah is God manifesting Himself to people in the Old Testament. This is best understood as God revealing Himself in the three-dimensional world. God is spirit, but not a three-dimensional ghost or fog. God is much like light—everywhere in a very real way, but undetectable unless He desires to be known.

Multidimensionality and God's Omnipresence, Omnipotence, and Omniscience

God's attributes that are unique to Him being God are: His being everywhere (omnipresent), His being all-powerful (omnipotent), and His being all-knowing (omniscient). These are characteristics of God that the human mind has a very difficult time comprehending.

Omnipresence. God is everywhere in all His creation.

> **Where can I go from Your Spirit? Or where can I flee from Your presence? If I ascend into heaven, You are there; If I make my bed in hell, behold, You are there. If I take the wings of the morning, and dwell in the uttermost parts of the sea, even there Your hand shall lead me, and Your right hand shall hold me. If I say, "Surely the darkness shall fall on me," even the night shall be light about me (Psalms 139:7-11).**

This passage speaks of God being like the full spectrum of light in that He is everywhere. But He is not an invisible force. He is an almighty being. Torrey makes the point that "God is in some places in a way he is not in other places."[169] Jesus is with the Father in heaven right now. The Holy Spirit indwells all believers. God is everywhere, but His essence as the various heads of the Trinity are concentrated in certain places rather than others. Jesus ascended to heaven to be at the right hand of the Father.[170] He had to ascend for the Spirit to come to earth.[171] Even though Jesus and the Father are in heaven, they indwell all believers through the Holy Spirit.

Omnipotence. This is God's attribute of being all-powerful. Torrey writes, "God can do all things; nothing is too hard for him; all things are possible with Him. God is omnipotent."[172] The greatest and most foundational example of God's unlimited power is His creation. God created from nothing the universe and all that is in it. "In the beginning God created the heavens and the earth" (Genesis 1:1). "Then God said, 'Let there be light'; and there was light" (Genesis 1:3). His extra dimensionality highlights God's omnipotence. In order to create three dimensions of space and one dimension of time, God must be outside of these four dimensions.

Omniscience. God is all-knowing. God knows everything, He is perfect in knowledge, and His knowledge is infinite. God can see all of time and knows what has happened, what is happening, and what will happen. Prophecy is the best example of God's omniscience. Since He knows exactly what will happen in the future, He can give people glimpses of certain events. This is to prove who God is and to substantiate the Bible as truth given to people from the grand programmer.

God even knows the possibilities of what might happen—events that could occur if certain choices are made. In 1 Samuel 23, David and his men are on the run from Saul and his army. David gets word that the Philistines are pillaging an Israelite town called Keilah. David inquires of the Lord whether to go and help the people of Keilah and attack the Philistines. God responds with an affirmative. "Then David inquired of the LORD once again. And the LORD answered him and said, 'Arise, go down to Keilah. For I will deliver the Philistines into your hand'" (1 Samuel 23:4). Thus, David and his men fight the Philistines and liberate the town of Keilah.

Saul hears of the battle between David and the Philistines and realizes that David and his men are in Keilah. Apparently, because of the location of the town, they are trapped; Saul has them potentially cornered. David fears that Saul will come to Keilah and wipe out the town in an attempt to kill him, so he inquires of the Lord again, asking two questions. He asks the Lord if Saul will even come down to Keilah to kill him. He also asks if the men of Keilah will surrender him and his men to Saul. The Lord answers David with an affirmative to both questions. "Will the men of Keilah deliver me into his hand? Will Saul come down, as Your servant has heard? O LORD God of Israel, I pray, tell Your servant. And the LORD said, 'He will come down.' Then David said, 'Will the men of Keilah deliver me and my men into the hand of Saul?' And the Lord said, 'They will deliver you'" (1 Samuel 23:11-12).

The next thing that happens in the story is very interesting. "So David and his men, about six hundred, arose and departed from Keilah and went wherever they could go. Then it was told Saul that David had escaped from Keilah; so he halted the expedition" (1 Samuel 23:13). The passage says that after David heard from the Lord about what was going to happen, he left Keilah and Saul did not attack. Both events that God foresaw as going to happen, never did take place. God can see what might happen, or what could happen if certain decisions are made. David changed the outcome by leaving Keilah.[173] God's omniscience transcends time in that He not only knows what is going to happen, but He also knows what could have happened. God must be outside of man's time and space for this to be possible.

Triunity and Multidimensionality

The Trinity is a fundamental doctrine of the Christian faith. It is clearly implied in the Bible that there are three godheads, Father, Son, and Holy Spirit. Though this is a basic doctrine, and though the doctrine is clearly taught in the Scriptures, the concept is still nearly impossible for a three-dimensional being to comprehend. Many attempts have been made to help mankind understand this incredibly difficult teaching using illustrations. Some have used water. Water can exist in three different states—a vapor, a liquid, and a solid—while still being water. Others have used the egg. An egg has three different parts: the yolk, the white, and the shell. Both illustrations still come up short in fully explaining the triunity of the godhead. Hugh Ross agrees that three-dimensional illustrations of God's triunity cannot adequately describe the godhead. Not only do they fail to properly explain the Trinity, but faulty examples can lead to doctrinal errors. Ross states:

> **All naturalistic, four-dimensional [Ross adds time as the fourth dimension] representations of the Trinity must reflect either tritheism or modalism. Our human frame of reference holds no other options. For that matter, all naturalistic, ten-dimensional representations of the Trinity will to a lesser extent fail too. The triune God, after all, has the power to create space-time dimensions at will.**[174]

He goes on to explain that even though the extra dimensions of string theory have enhanced man's understanding of the triunity of God, it is still not fully comprehended by people.

Returning once again to Flatland and the two-dimensional footprints, Flatman lives in a two-dimensional plane. He sees what appears to him as four objects in his two-dimensional world.

Figure 8.1. Two-dimensional footprints.

If Flatman were to look at these manifestations that appear in his two-dimensional realm, he could easily think they were four different objects, but he could not be more wrong. The four objects are all part of the same person. They appear to Flatman as four separate objects, but they are not. Could Flatman understand this? What if someone told him that these four objects are really one? Would he or could he believe them? In a rudimentary and much simpler sense, this is the case with the triunity of God. Three manifestations of God exist in the three-dimensional world and thinking, but God is one—a Trinity of Father, Son, and Holy Spirit.

Chapter 9

Angels and Demons

I was practically an atheist in my childhood. Science was what led me to the conclusion that the world is much more complex than we can explain. I can only explain the mystery of existence to myself by the Supernatural.

–Allan Sandage (1926-2010), American astronomer, calculated the rate at which the universe expands and its age by observing distant stars

Nearly everyone has heard of angels. When the word *angel* is mentioned, most have some idea of what an angel is, or at least their personal perception of an angel. Beliefs about what angels are and do vary widely among people across the world. Movies, books, and television shows have all impacted what people think and understand about angels, so much of what people believe is not biblical. Pictures of angels as chubby little babies with wings and harps floating in a cloud are believed to come from Roman or Greek mythology. People do not turn into angels, nor do angels have halos or get their wings when a bell rings, according to the Bible.

Spiritual beings are part of nearly all major religions. An angel named Gabriel is said to have visited Muhammad in 610 AD. Gabriel, speaking on behalf of Allah, supposedly gave Muhammad the material that makes up their holy book, the Koran. "Koran is Arabic for 'the recitation,' and refers to the collection of revelations supposedly given by Allah through his archangel to Muhammad and preserved as the Islamic scripture."[175] The question from a biblical and Christian perspective is whether or not Muhammad encountered a real angel or the story is fabricated. If Muhammad encountered an authentic angel, then was it a good angel or an evil angel posing as one of God's holy messengers?

An angel named Moroni is said to have visited Joseph Smith, the father of Mormonism.

> **In 1820 Joseph Smith, Jr. claimed a heavenly vision that he said singled him out as the Lord's anointed prophet for this dispensation, though it was not until 1823, with the appearance of the angel Moroni at the quaking Smith's bedside, that Joe began his relationship to the fabulous 'golden plates,' or what was to become the *Book of Mormon*.**[176]

Once again, was Joseph really visited by an angel, or was it made up? If an angel visited him, was it a good or evil one? "But even if we, or an angel from heaven, preach any other gospel to you than what we have preached to you, let him be accursed" (Galatians 1:8). "And no wonder! For Satan himself transforms himself into an angel of light" (2 Corinthians 11:14). Examining the teachings of the Koran and the Book of Mormon will reveal fundamental and doctrinal disagreements with the Bible. That would lead one to believe that the angelic events were fabricated or delivered by a messenger of Satan. Either way, angels play an important role even in the beginnings of Islam and Mormonism.

Angels play an important role in the story of the Bible. The Bible tells of the existence and activities of angels from Genesis to Revelation. In the Scriptures, angels are taken for granted and assumed to be real beings. Many truths can be learned from studying angels as they appear and minister in the Bible. Even among literal biblical scholars, a wide variety of beliefs exist concerning angels, their appearing, their ministry, the fall into sin by many angels, and many other beliefs. Since no text gives a complete teaching about angels, scholars must look at the actions of these spiritual messengers to attempt to understand them better. The *Holman Bible Dictionary* states, "The text may focus on the service done or on the God served but rarely on the servants themselves. As a result we are left with a multitude of questions about the angelic host. Many of the most common questions asked about angels have no clear answers in Scripture. The nature of the angelic host is at best hinted at indirectly."[177] Angels are interesting beings, especially for the topic of spiritual dimensions because they are mentioned so many times in the Bible. The purpose of this chapter is to better understand angels in light of higher dimensions by looking at the Bible.

Angels Are Spiritual Beings

Angels are spiritual beings that sometimes appear as material beings. William Evans writes concerning angels, "They are spiritual beings. Hebrews 1:14 – 'Are they not all ministering spirits?' Psalm 104:4 – 'Who maketh his angels spirits; his ministers a flaming fire.' ...Although the angels are 'spirits,' they nevertheless oft-times have appeared to men invisible, and even human, form (Genesis 19; Judges 2:1; 6:11-22; Matthew 1:20; Luke 1:26; John 20:12)."[178]

Most of the time, people think of angels as having the ability to appear and then disappear. Not much thought is given to where angels are or where they go when they disappear. If angels are in God's presence, where is that place? Many believe that angels are all around them as invisible spirits. But after learning about the possibilities of higher dimensions that are also called spiritual dimensions, could angels be coming and going from the spiritual realm to the three-dimensional world? The answer is, most certainly. Science claims that there are more spatial dimensions than the three in which people live. These higher spatial dimensions are where angels, God, heaven, and hell are located. When angels enter the physical realm, they appear as three-dimensional beings. Angels are not floating around people as invisible spirits; they are right next to a person's three-dimensional world. Angels are only a millimeter away. When they are permitted to step into the physical realm, they appear. When they return to their spiritual realm, they disappear. The angels that appeared to the shepherds the night Christ was born are an example of angels appearing, then going back into the spiritual realm in Luke 2:8-15:

> **Now there were in the same country shepherds living out in the fields, keeping watch over their flock by night. And behold, an angel of the Lord stood before them, and the glory of the Lord shone around them, and they were greatly afraid. Then the angel said to them, "Do not be afraid, for behold, I bring you good tidings of great joy which will be to all people. For there is born to you this day in the city of David a Savior, who is Christ the Lord. And this will be the sign to you: You will find a Babe wrapped in swaddling cloths, lying in a manger." And suddenly**

> **there was with the angel a multitude of the heavenly host praising God and saying: "Glory to God in the highest, And on earth peace, goodwill toward men!" So it was, when the angels had gone away from them into heaven, that the shepherds said to one another, "Let us now go to Bethlehem and see this thing that has come to pass, which the Lord has made known to us."**

The verses describe the angels entering the shepherd's three-dimensional realm, then leaving their realm, "Suddenly there was a multitude of angels...as the angels were gone away from them into heaven." The best explanation for the sudden appearance of angels is their inhabiting the spiritual realm and entering the physical realm when God allowed.

Another example of angels entering the physical dimension is the story of Zacharias in the gospel of Luke. An angel appears to Zacharias to announce that his wife would be having a baby, who would be John the Baptist. "Then an angel of the Lord appeared to him, standing on the right side of the altar of incense" (Luke 1:11). Zacharias sees the angel and is afraid initially, until the angel calms his fears. The angel introduces himself as Gabriel. "And the angel answered and said to him, 'I am Gabriel, who stands in the presence of God, and was sent to speak to you and bring you these glad tidings'" (Luke 1:19). The angel appears to Zacharias while he is in the temple—and he came from the spiritual dimension directly into the temple where Zacharias was serving.

An Old Testament example of angels entering the physical dimension is found in Genesis chapter nineteen. Two angels visit Lot to warn him of the impending destruction coming upon Sodom and Gomorrah and tell him to get out before it happens.

> **Now the two angels came to Sodom in the evening, and Lot was sitting in the gate of Sodom. When Lot saw them, he rose to meet them, and he bowed himself with his face toward the ground. And he said, "Here now, my lords, please turn in to your servant's house and spend the night, and wash your feet; then you may rise early and go on your way." And they said, "No, but we will spend the night in the open square." But he insisted strongly; so they turned in to him and entered his house. Then he made them a feast, and baked unleavened bread, and they ate (Genesis 19:1-3).**

Here the angels appear as men and eat food like men do. Some scholars will interpret passages such as this one as teaching that angels, which are spirit beings, must take over a physical body to inhabit the physical world. This passage is used as an example, along with the accounts of Satan appearing as a serpent and the demons asking Jesus if they could enter the swine. The best answer from a spiritual dimension aspect is that when angels enter the physical realm from the spiritual realm, they appear three-dimensional. They have three-dimensional bodies, just like any three-dimensional being would have. In this passage the angels appear so much like men, no one can tell the difference. If the Bible did not tell the reader they were angels; they would be understood to be men.

Angels, Good and Evil

Two major divisions of angels are found in the Bible, good and evil. The Bible reveals that two groups of spiritual beings are in conflict with one another. Daniel highlights this angelic conflict:

> **Then he said to me, "Do not fear, Daniel, for from the first day that you set your heart to understand, and to humble yourself before your God, your words were heard; and I have come because of your words. But the prince of the kingdom of Persia withstood me twenty-one days; and behold, Michael, one of the chief princes, came to help me, for I had been left alone there with the kings of Persia. Now I have come to make you understand what will happen to your people in the latter days, for the vision refers to many days yet to come" (Daniel 10:12-14).**

Here Daniel is speaking with an angel who came to give him a message. The angel speaks about another angel that hindered him from arriving for twenty-one days. One angel is called the Prince of Persia, while another angel that came to assist is called Michael, a chief prince. These two groups of angels battle one another. We see good angels that have remained loyal to God, serving and worshiping Him, as well as evil angels that neither serve nor worship God but attempt to hinder the work of God on earth. This is a clear indication of higher dimensions. The battle of angels did not take place in the visible three-dimensional world; it was in a higher dimension, right next to the three-dimensional world. It indicates the presence of a vast higher dimensional spiritual realm, which is the most reasonable explanation of the passage.

Satan is the leader of the evil angels, also called fallen angels. Satan is referred to as an angel in 2 Corinthians 11:14 and as a cherub (classification of an angel) in Ezekiel 28:14. Therefore, Satan is a created being. As an angel, he is multidimensional. In the garden, where he appeared to Eve, he is called a serpent. Spirit beings are also assembled under the leadership of Satan, working against man, God and Jesus Christ. They are called evil spirits: "And that very hour He cured many of infirmities, afflictions, and *evil spirits;* and to many blind He gave sight" [emphasis added] (Luke 7:21). They are also called unclean spirits: "And when He had called His twelve disciples to Him, He gave them power over *unclean spirits,* to cast them out, and to heal all kinds of sickness and all kinds of disease" [emphasis added] (Matthew 10:1). They are also called devils in the King James Version: "So the *devils* besought him, saying, If thou cast us out, suffer us to go away into the herd of swine" [emphasis added] (Matthew 8:31); and they are called demons, "So the *demons* begged Him, saying, 'If You cast us out, permit us to go away into the herd of swine'" [emphasis added] (Matthew 8:31). Many scholars understand these terms to be interchangeable with angel—referring to an evil angel, of course.

Though much is not understood about evil angels, demons, unclean spirits, or evil spirits, they are real beings that have crossed over into the three-dimensional world. They manifest themselves in various ways by attacking people in the three-dimensional realm, even though they are from the spiritual realm. They can cross into the physical dimension somehow.

The good angels are those that worship and serve the Lord. They minister to people on God's behalf. Angels delivered news to Mary and Joseph concerning Jesus' birth and later communicated to them the necessity of going to Egypt as well as returning to Israel (Matthew 1:20, 24; 2:13, 19; Luke 1:26-38). Angels protected people: "My God sent His angel and shut the lions' mouths, so that they have not hurt me, because I was found innocent before Him; and also, O king, I have done no wrong before you" (Daniel 6:22). Angels ministered to Jesus after He was tempted by Satan: "And He was there in the wilderness forty days, tempted by Satan, and was with the wild beasts; and the angels ministered to Him" (Mark 1:13). Angels execute judgment on behalf of God: "Then immediately an angel of the Lord struck him, because he did not give glory to God. And he was eaten by worms and died" (Acts 12:23). Angels announced Jesus' resurrection: "And she saw two angels in white sitting, one at the head and the other at the feet, where the body of Jesus had lain. Then they said to her, 'Woman, why are you weeping?' She said to them, 'Because they have taken away my Lord, and I do not know where they have laid Him'" (John 20:12-13). Angels announced Jesus' ascension:

> **Now when He had spoken these things, while they watched, He was taken up, and a cloud received Him out of their sight. And while they looked steadfastly toward heaven as He went up, behold, two men stood by them in white apparel, who also said, "Men of Galilee, why do you stand gazing up into heaven? This same Jesus, who was taken up from you into heaven, will so come in like manner as you saw Him go into heaven" (Acts 1:9-11).**

In all these examples, angels ministered in the physical realm. Though angels are spirit beings and dwell in the spiritual dimensions, they work on behalf of God in the three-dimensional realm.

The "sons of God"

One of the oddest passages that supports the cross-dimensional movements of angels is in Genesis 6:1-7. In this passage it appears to be teaching that angels cohabited on earth with people and even reproduced with human women to have an offspring that was totally different than anything before. In this passage, spirit beings appear as material beings, having human bodies and living in the three-dimensional world.

> **Now it came to pass, when men began to multiply on the face of the earth, and daughters were born to them, that the sons of God saw the daughters of men, that they *were* beautiful; and they took wives for themselves of all whom they chose. And the LORD said, "My Spirit shall not strive with man forever, for he *is* indeed flesh; yet his days shall be one hundred and twenty years." There were giants on the earth in those days, and also afterward, when the sons of God came in to the daughters of men and they bore *children* to them. Those *were* the mighty men who *were* of old, men of renown. Then the LORD saw that the wickedness of man *was* great in the earth, and *that* every intent of the thoughts of his heart *was* only evil continually. And the LORD was sorry that He had made man on the earth, and He was grieved in His heart. So the LORD said, "I will destroy man whom I have created from the face of the earth, both man and beast, creeping thing and birds of the air, for I am sorry that I have made them." (Genesis 6:1-7)**

In the account of Noah's flood, where the entire face of the earth is covered in water and destroyed, the Bible identifies an intriguing group of men called the "sons of God." This passage begins by pointing out that the "sons of God" are having relations with a group of women called the "daughters of men." As a result of this union between the sons of God and the daughters of men, giants were born. The word that is translated "giants" in the NKJV and KJV is translated or transliterated as Nephilim in other Bible translations. Various views exist as to who these "sons of God" are, and who their offspring, the Nephilim, are. The *Tyndale Concise Bible Commentary* offers three options regarding who these sons of God could be:

> **The "sons of God" mentioned in Genesis 6:2 have been identified in three different ways: (1) as Seth's apostate descendants who intermarried with the depraved descendants of Cain, (2) as fallen angels who took on physical bodies to cohabit with women of the human race, and (3) as despotic chieftains of Cainite descent who married a plurality of wives in order to expand their dominion.**[179]

The commentary goes on to suggest which of the three options they lean toward. "Although each of the three views has its problems, those of the 'angel' view can be most satisfactorily resolved."[180]

Who are these offspring called Nephilim? The word *Nephilim* is used only twice in the Old Testament, here in Genesis 6:2 and in Numbers 13:33 where the Israelites comment that they felt like grasshoppers in their sight. Therefore, these Nephilim were large men or giant men. The Septuagint translated the word *Nephilim* as *gìgantes*, the Greek word for giants. The *Holman Bible Dictionary* defines Nephilim as the following:

> **Nephilim: Term probably derived from the root "to fall" and meaning either "the fallen ones" or else "ones who fall [violently] upon others." At Genesis 6:4 the term designates ancient heroes who, according to most interpreters, are the products of sexual union of heavenly beings ("sons of God"; compare Job 1:6, 2:1, 38:7; Psalm 29:1, 82:6) and human women. The account illustrates the breakdown of the God-ordained order separating heaven and earth (Genesis 1:6-10) and specifying reproduction "each according to its kind" (1:11-12, 21, 24-25). God intervened to reestablish limits inherent in creation (6:3; compare 3:22-23). At Numbers 13:33 Nephilim designates a race of giants descended from Anak against whom the Israelites appeared as grasshoppers.**[181]

In this passage, evil, fallen angels demonstrate human qualities to the point that procreation with another human is possible. This raises more questions than answers, but it seems to be the correct exposition of the biblical text. Fallen angels enter the three-dimensional world from the spiritual dimension, have relations with human women, and the offspring created are called Nephilim. As extraordinary as this sounds, many fundamental Bible scholars hold to this view, even though it defies any conventional, three-dimensional explanation. The only way this passage makes sense is believing in the spiritual realm. John MacArthur interprets the "sons of God" in this passage as fallen angels, and he writes:

> **Satan and his angels had already rebelled and been thrown out of heaven and eternally fixed in a state of unmixed wickedness. Satan had been successful in**

> **the Garden and his demonic force had been at work motivating corruption in the world. The Genesis 6 account was perhaps the most heinous effort they made related to the God-ordained provision of marriage (v. 1). The demons mounted an attack on marriage and procreation that wickedly influenced subsequent generations.[182]**

This was Satan's revolt and attempt to disrupt God's plan on earth of bringing a Savior through Eve's lineage. Somehow, Satan saw an opportunity to corrupt the bloodlines of men on earth. In Genesis 6:9, the Bible says, "...Noah was a just man, perfect in his generations. Noah walked with God." The phrase "perfect in his generations" seems to indicate that Noah's lineage or bloodline had not been corrupted by the fallen angels.

The problem of how a spiritual being, from the spiritual realm, can procreate with a human is difficult to reckon theologically or even logically for that matter. MacArthur writes:

> **That certainly raises the question: How can spirit beings marry women? It is possible only if they dwell in human bodies, as angels can and have done (cf. Genesis 18:1-2, 8; 19:1, 5; Hebrews 13:2). Those demons entered men's bodies (a phenomenon frequently encountered by Christ and the apostles in the Gospel record), as is clear from the children who were born from those unions (Genesis 6:4). Though the children were human, there was a pervasive influence on them from the demons.[183]**

John MacArthur solves the problem by understanding that the sons of God were fallen angels or demon spirits, and they possessed the men. The offspring of the union, called Nephilim, were somehow affected by the demonic possession of their fathers genetically. Other scholars, such as Chuck Missler, understand the sons of God to be angels themselves and not demons possessing human bodies (also believed by this author). Though angels are generally hidden from a person's sight, they also appear as men. The writer of Hebrews claims that it is possible to entertain a stranger that is actually an angel.[184] Angels do appear as men in the Old Testament[185]—they eat food,[186] and engage in physical combat.[187] According to a literal exposition of the passage, angels cohabitating with women seems to be the correct view. Chuck Missler lists some of the many scholars that support the angel view:

> **It should also be pointed out that most conservative Bible scholars accept the "angel" view. Among those supporting the "angel" view are: G. H. Pember, M. R. DeHaan, C. H. McIntosh, F. Delitzsch, A. C. Gaebelein, A. W. Pink, Donald Grey Barnhouse, Henry Morris, Merril F. Unger, Arnold Fruchtenbaum, Hal Lindsey, and Chuck Smith, being among the best known.**[188]

Understanding that the "sons of God" were angels who chose to leave their spiritual realm and live on earth, marrying women, can help explain two obscure passages in Jude and 2 Peter.

> **And the angels which kept not their first estate, but left their own habitation, he hath reserved in everlasting chains under darkness unto the judgment of the great day. Even as Sodom and Gomorrah, and the cities about them in like manner, giving themselves over to fornication, and going after strange flesh, are set forth for an example, suffering the vengeance of eternal fire (Jude 6-7 KJV).**

In this passage, Jude writes about some angels that "did not keep their first estate but left their own habitation." The Greek word for *estate* in this passage is translated *beginning* forty times in the New Testament.[189] This is meaning the angels' origin, their original beginning place. The Greek word for *habitation* is used only twice in the New Testament and is translated *house* the other time it is used.[190] "For in this we groan, earnestly desiring to be clothed upon with our house which is from heaven" (2 Corinthians 5:2 KJV). The word translated *house* in this verse is another way of saying *body, a heavenly body.* In Jude 6 the angels did not maintain their original spiritual bodies but left them to become three-dimensional. Jude continues to explain that the angels gave themselves over to fornication and went after strange flesh. The word *strange* means *different or other or another.* Many Bible scholars, including this author, believe that this verse is talking about the angels in Genesis chapter six. They left their higher-dimensional spiritual realm, lived in the three-dimensional realm and had sexual relations with human women. As a result, Jude says, that these angels are "reserved in everlasting chains under darkness unto the judgment of the great day." They are in spiritual prison.

Another passage connected to Genesis 6 is 2 Peter 2:4-6:

> **For if God did not spare the angels who sinned, but cast them down to hell and delivered *them* into chains of darkness, to be reserved for judgment; and did not spare the ancient world, but saved Noah, *one of* eight *people*, a preacher of righteousness, bringing in the flood on the world of the ungodly; and turning the cities of Sodom and Gomorrah into ashes,**

condemned *them* to destruction, making *them* an example to those who afterward would live ungodly.

In this passage, Peter identifies angels that sinned and have been "delivered into chains of darkness, to be reserved for judgment." This again points to the "sons of God" in the Genesis 6 account.

Even though conservative Bible scholars are divided on exactly what is taking place in Genesis 6, something cross-dimensional is happening. Spiritual beings are entering the physical, three-dimensional world. Taken with Jude 6-7 and 2 Peter 2:4-6, they were not only crossing into the physical realm, but they had sexual relations with women. This is possible only if the angels fully entered the three-dimensional realm as physical beings.

Chapter 10

Jesus: God in the Game

Jesus knows our world. He does not disdain us like the God of Aristotle. We can speak to Him and He answers us. Although He is a person like ourselves, He is God and transcends all things.

–Alexis Carrel, Nobel Laureate in Medicine and Physiology

The supreme miracle for Christians is the Resurrection. Something happened to those few men who knew Jesus, which led them to believe that Jesus yet lived, with such intensity and conviction that this belief remains the basis of the Christian Church two thousand years later.

–Sir Nevill Mott (1905-1996), received the 1977 Nobel Prize in Physics for his research on the magnetic and electrical properties of non-crystalline semiconductors

Mankind lives in a digital, three-dimensional universe created and sustained by a grand programmer. Though the universe and humanity was created perfect, sin entered the world. If one were to describe the world a person lives in as digital and simulated, then sin entering would be like a computer virus taking root in the three-dimensional world, affecting all that is within it. God's remedy for a person's sin-virus is Jesus Christ. As a result of the sin-virus, people became spiritually dead and separated from God. If a person were to remain in that condition until their physical death, they would be separated forever. God decided to enter the simulation Himself to save people from the sin-virus, so He entered the three-dimensional world as Jesus Christ. He came as a three-dimensional man to pay for mankind's sins, offering an eternal cure.

God coming to earth as a man allowed individuals to be born from a perfect genealogy once again. When Adam and Eve sinned, they caused everyone born to them to be born sinners (Romans 3:23). Mankind's bloodline was corrupt. The sin-virus corrupted humanity's spiritual existence, and it even affected their physical existence. Everyone who has ever lived since Adam and Eve was born in sin, separated from God. Everyone, that is, except Jesus Christ (2 Corinthians 5:21; Hebrews 7:26). God chose to enter the world as the new or last Adam, a perfect man. "And so it is written, 'The first man Adam became a living being.' The last Adam *became* a life-giving spirit" (1 Corinthians 15:45). Jesus had perfect blood, untainted by sin. He lived the perfect life and died on the cross to pay for mankind's sin. Therefore, a person must be born again. Not born of the first Adam, but born of the last Adam, Jesus Christ, God in the flesh.

> **Jesus answered and said to him, "Most assuredly, I say to you, unless one is born again, he cannot see the kingdom of God." Nicodemus said to Him, "How can a man be born when he is old? Can he enter a second time into his mother's womb and be born?" Jesus answered, "Most assuredly, I say to you, unless one is born of water and the Spirit, he cannot enter the kingdom of God. That which is born of the flesh is flesh, and that which is born of the Spirit is spirit. Do not marvel that I said to you, 'You must be born again'" (John 3:3-7).**

A person needs new blood, a new genealogy through the last

Adam, through Jesus Christ, God's Son. When a person accepts Jesus as God in the flesh and Savior of mankind, that individual has a new lineage. The person is spiritually born through Christ and directly related again to the Father.

God entering the three-dimensional universe as Jesus Christ is the greatest example and proof of a higher dimension. If God, who exists outside of man's space and time dimensions, enters into the three-dimensional world as a human, He came from someplace. This chapter will look at God, existing outside of space and time, becoming three-dimensional and living with people on earth.

The Incarnation of Jesus Christ

The almighty God that created the universe and all that is within it came to earth born of a woman. If there was any doubt as to whether Jesus was God before being born in Bethlehem, John repudiates it in the first few verses of his gospel account. "In the beginning was the Word, and the Word was with God, and the Word was God. He was in the beginning with God. All things were made through Him, and without Him nothing was made that was made" (John 1:1-3). John continues a few verses farther, "And the Word became flesh and dwelt among us, and we beheld His glory, the glory as of the only begotten of the Father, full of grace and truth" (John 1:14). These verses were written by the Apostle John to refute any teaching that Jesus did not exist before being born physically. Jesus is the eternal God who came to earth as a man. God who existed in the spiritual dimension, entered the physical realm, crossing over into mankind's three-dimensional world.

Paul also confirms that Jesus was God in the flesh. "But when the fullness of the time had come, God sent forth His Son, born of a woman, born under the law" (Galatians 4:4). Paul declares that Jesus, being born of a woman, is called God's Son because Jesus was born physically of the Holy Spirit. God entered the world physically through birth. "And without controversy great is the mystery of godliness: God was manifested in the flesh, justified in the Spirit, seen by angels, preached among the Gentiles, believed on in the world, received up in glory" (1 Timothy 3:16). Here Paul clearly states that God was manifest in the flesh. The Greek word used for *manifested* can be translated *appear* or *appeared.* It is translated *appear* or *appearing* twelve times in the New Testament.[191] Therefore, the God outside of space and time appeared in the flesh as Jesus Christ.

God limited His dimensionality to become human. He was born and grew as a man, then His body was both put to death, and then raised as a resurrected body. For Jesus to be born, Mary was impregnated by the Holy Spirit. "Now the birth of Jesus Christ was as follows: After His mother Mary was betrothed to Joseph, before they came together, she was found with child of the Holy Spirit" (Matthew 1:18). Jesus was born without sin, not because of who Mary was, but because of the Holy Spirit impregnating Mary. Mary was a sinner, just like all others born to Adam (Romans 3:23, 5:12). How is it possible for Jesus to be born sinless from the body of Mary? That question requires a multidimensional answer to a three-dimensional mind, which is very difficult for most to comprehend. John MacArthur admits to this difficulty of understanding:

> **Obviously Jesus' conception by the Holy Spirit is a great mystery. Even had He wanted to do so, how could God have explained to us, in terms we could comprehend, how such a blending of the divine and human could have been accomplished? We could no more fathom such a thing than we can fathom God's creating the universe from nothing, His being one God in three Persons, or His giving an entirely new spiritual nature to those who trust in His Son.**[192]

The incarnation of Jesus Christ is God coming to the physical world through being born of a virgin. The three-dimensional view is the only part a person can comprehend. A baby being born is not a unique phenomenon. The immaterial creator of the universe coming into the three-dimensional world? That is much more dramatic. This is precisely what the Bible teaches; God was born in Bethlehem and named Jesus. The grand programmer made His entrance into the digital, three-dimensional universe of mankind, and the world celebrates this event at Christmas every December 25th.

The Life of Jesus Christ

Jesus' earthly ministry is evidence of both His humanity and divinity. Jesus' humanity is usually never questioned, and it is normally easily understood. A person's three-dimensional mind has a difficult time reconciling the creator of the universe in a human body. As a result, Jesus becomes in the human mind a super-human being that has god-like powers to do whatever He wants. Jesus can be seen only as a powerful man and not as the eternal, omniscient, omnipotent, and omnipresent creator of the universe. However, Jesus was fully God and fully human.

Jesus displayed characteristics and evidence of his Human nature:

- Jesus grew, just as any young child would grow in an earthly body. “And Jesus increased in wisdom and stature, and in favor with God and men” (Luke 2:52).
- Jesus displayed hunger. “And when He had fasted forty days and forty nights, afterward He was hungry” (Matthew 4:2).
- Jesus displayed thirst. “After this, Jesus, knowing that all things were now accomplished, that the Scripture might be fulfilled, said, ‘I thirst!’” (John 19:28).
- Jesus became physically tired. “Now Jacob’s well was there. Jesus therefore, being wearied from *His* journey, sat thus by the well. It was about the sixth hour.” (John 4:6).
- Jesus displayed sorrow by crying. “Jesus wept” (John 11:35).
- Jesus displayed characteristics and evidences of His divine nature:
- Jesus claimed to exist from eternity past. “Jesus said to them, ‘Most assuredly, I say to you, before Abraham

was, I AM'" (John 8:58).

- Jesus received and did not refuse worship due only to God. "And behold, a leper came and worshiped Him, saying, 'Lord, if You are willing, You can make me clean.' Then Jesus put out *His* hand and touched him, saying, 'I am willing; be cleansed.' Immediately his leprosy was cleansed" (Matthew 8:2-3).
- Jesus claims to be God and has authority over the sabbath. "For the Son of man is Lord even of the Sabbath" (Matthew 12:8).
- Jesus is recognized as God by the demons. "Saying, 'Let *us* alone! What have we to do with You, Jesus of Nazareth? Did You come to destroy us? I know who You are—the Holy One of God!'" (Mark 1:24).
- Jesus forgave sins. The Pharisees understood that only God could do that.

When He saw their faith, He said to him, "Man, your sins are forgiven you." And the scribes and the Pharisees began to reason, saying, "Who is this who speaks blasphemies? Who can forgive sins but God alone?" But when Jesus perceived their thoughts, He answered and said to them, "Why are you reasoning in your hearts? Which is easier, to say, 'Your sins are forgiven you,' or to say, 'Rise up and walk'? But that you may know that the Son of Man has power on earth to forgive sins" —He said to the man who was paralyzed, "I say to you, arise, take up your bed, and go to your house." Immediately he rose up before them, took up what he had been lying on, and departed to his own house, glorifying God. (Luke 5:20-25).

The ministry of Jesus Christ is marked by hundreds, if not thousands, of miracles that are not explainable in the three-dimensional world. Jesus performed various miracles during His three years of ministry to proclaim and demonstrate that He was indeed God in the flesh. Proving yourself to be God in the flesh would be a grand task for anyone to accomplish. If a person were to make such a claim, others would certainly ask for proof. Jesus performed many miraculous signs and wonders to prove He was the creator of the physical world. All of these miracles were intentionally directed at showing He had power over the curse of sin on mankind and the world. Jesus held power to reverse and even do away with the sin-virus that infected mankind and the world. Many of Jesus' signs involved overcoming laws of the three-dimensional realm. Some of these laws were a result of the sin-virus entering the three-dimensional realm—miracles such as healing the sick, raising the dead, providing food for the hungry, and calming a storm. Sickness, death, working for food, and destructive weather all result from sin entering the physical world in Genesis chapter three.

Let's once again use the example of a digital video game world. The creator of the digital world, though he has entered the digital world he created, can override or supersede the rules placed upon the characters in the three-dimensional world. Jesus, in order to prove He was the creator of the three-dimensional world, performed acts not governed by the dimensional rules or laws of the physical world. John lists several important signs in his gospel that demonstrate Jesus' divinity. He changes water into wine (2:1-11), heals the nobleman's son (4:46-54), heals the paralytic man (5:1-16), feeds the 5,000 (6:1-14), walks on water (6:15-21), heals the man born blind (9:1-11), raises Lazarus from the dead (11:1-27), and is resurrected from the dead Himself (20:1-29). The miracles of Jesus are best explained using multidimensions, even though the explanation cannot be totally understood by the three-dimensional mind. Miracles are not logical in the three-dimensional world of laws and rules. Granville writes in his book, *The Fourth Dimension and the Bible:*

> **One reason why some very good people hesitate about accepting the miracles of the Bible at their face value is that they assume that such miracles can only be brought about by violating or in some way interfering with the laws of nature, the laws governing our three-dimensional universe. This difficulty vanishes if instead we look upon the miracles of the Bible as the perfectly logical results of the working out of laws connected with higher spaces, laws which include the lower, the so-called natural laws of our material universe, just as our space is contained within the higher spaces. We may then consider the miracles performed by Jesus, the apostles and the prophets to consist of momentary revelations by God to mortals of the operations of some of those higher laws of which we are as yet ignorant.**[193]

God can influence the rules and laws in the three-dimensional world to accomplish something that is impossible for people to do in three dimensions. The life of Christ presents a multidimensional God who became three-dimensional in a human body. God left His heavenly home to come to earth in human flesh.

The Death and Resurrection of Jesus Christ

The birth of Christ was God entering the three-dimensional world. The death and resurrection of Christ is God overcoming the curse of sin while presenting a resurrected body demonstrating the ability to move into and out of man's three dimensions of space. Jesus confined Himself to specific rules and laws in His human body of flesh, but His resurrected body was governed by a new set of rules and laws. He had a material body but was able to enter a room without opening a door (John 20:19-24). Many scholars and commentators have a difficult time explaining how Jesus entered a locked room. Some even refer to Jesus having a spirit body that can pass through walls or solid objects, but Jesus demonstrated to His troubled disciples that He was not a ghost or a spirit by permitting them to touch Him.

> **And He said to them, "Why are you troubled? And why do doubts arise in your hearts? Behold My hands and My feet, that it is I Myself. Handle Me and see, for a spirit does not have flesh and bones as you see I have." When He had said this, He showed them His hands and His feet (Luke 24:38-40).**

Jesus also showed He was not a spirit by eating food with them. "But while they still did not believe for joy, and marveled, He said to them, 'Have you any food here?' So they gave Him a piece of a broiled fish and some honeycomb. And He took it and ate in their presence" (Luke 24:41-43). Arthur Willink comments on Jesus' resurrection appearance from a higher dimensional view:

> **So with regard to His appearance on the same evening, and on that day week; there is no call to speak of**

entering the room through a closed door, in virtue of an indefinable property with which His Risen Body has been conjecturally invested. He simply passed from that spot in the Higher Space which adjoined the spot in the room which He wished to occupy, and so coming from the Unseen, He stood in the midst of His Disciples, finding no obstacle of any kind before Him. And in like manner He departed from them.[194]

He also showed His scarred hands and side to Thomas (John 20:26-29). He was breaking bread with two disciples and then vanished from their sight (Luke 24:30-31). Willink writes, "Thus there is no difficulty in perceiving how it was that at Emmaus He vanished out of the sight of the two Disciples. He simply passed along the unseen path into the Higher Space, where their eyes could not follow Him."[195]

Jesus' resurrected body had similarities to His earthly body, but there were distinct differences also. Paul writes to the Corinthian believers about the resurrected bodies of believers being different than their fleshly bodies (1 Corinthians 15:35-50). Paul, again to the Corinthians in a later letter, writes about the new body a believer will have in heaven—a heavenly body made by God (2 Corinthians 5:1-8).

The resurrection and resurrected bodies are what a person will need to live in the spiritual dimension. The spiritual dimension must be a real place with spatial dimensions and locality, for Christ and all believers will have real material bodies, though they will be perfected and without sin. Our struggle as three-dimensional beings to picture resurrected believers living in the spiritual realm causes us to think of the spiritual realm like a hazy dream. However, it is more real than the physical, three-dimensional world.

Jesus Christ's ascension is yet another display of His multidimensionality after the resurrection. After giving the disciples their final commission, known today as the Great Commission, Jesus ascends into heaven—He departed into the next realm, the spiritual realm. The disciples saw Him go into another dimension. According to Willink, their description is consistent with a possible departure into the next dimension. He writes:

> **When the time came for the departure of the Lord from the Earth, He did not leave His Disciples as at other times after His Resurrection, but in such a way as that it should be clear to them that His departure was definite, and that they should see Him no more among them as before. Therefore having taken them with Him to Mount Olivet, He rose from the Earth for a certain distance, not so far as to disappear gradually, but apparently only a short way, and then a cloud veiled Him from their sight, and under cover of the cloud He passed into the Higher Space, to appear on earth no more. While from the Higher Space two "men" came forth, fulfilled their message to the Disciples, and departed as they had come, entering into the Higher Space again.**[196]

Jesus Christ is the ultimate example of a higher-dimensional being entering the three-dimensional world. The creator of the digital world, the maker of all atoms and molecules, came into the simulation to save mankind from the sin-virus. Jesus Christ being God in the flesh is what sets Christianity apart from all other religions. In all other religions, people are attempting to get to God through good works or personal merit of some kind. Christianity is God coming to mankind, seeking a relationship with every person. God not only came to mankind, but He pays the person's way to an eternal relationship with Him. To make this happen, God entered the world as a man, died for mankind's sins, and offered salvation as a free gift of grace to all who would receive Him as God in the flesh and Savior.

Chapter 11

Back to the Future: It's About Time!

From His true dominion it follows that the true God is a living, intelligent and powerful Being; and from His other perfections, that He is supreme, or most perfect. He is eternal and infinite, omnipotent and omniscient; that is, His duration reaches from eternity to eternity; His presence from infinity to infinity; He governs all things, and knows all things that are or can be done.

–Sir Isaac Newton (1642-1727), founder of Classical Physics and Infinitesimal Calculus

The funeral of a family member or a person that one knows well illustrates the separation of body and spirit. The body is visibly present in the casket, but there is no life in the body. Before death, the individual had a personality and emotions that were part of who that person was known to be. But in the casket, the person lies lifeless and still before living relatives and friends, as if in a deep sleep. The person's consciousness or spirit has left its earthly body and entered the spiritual dimension. Because it is customary to see a body melded with its consciousness so tightly that they appear as one inseparable unit, seeing a lifeless body is difficult to comprehend mentally. As stated in an earlier chapter, the body is like a computer shell or hardware and a person's spirit is like the software. In the same way that the hardware houses the software or internal programming so that the computer functions correctly, the body houses the spirit until the body physically dies, releasing the spirit to the spiritual dimension.

The Bible states that the spirit will go to one of two separate destinations after the body dies. When the body ceases to function and the spirit is released to the next dimension, the two options are heaven or hell. Heaven is the place designed by God as His dwelling place, and it is also the dwelling place for good angels and for believers. Hell is designed by God as the future habitation for Satan and his angels and demons. In hell, they will be separated from God and heaven and also prevented from negatively impacting heaven and those dwelling there. In this next section, heaven and hell will be viewed as real places with locality. We will also examine time and eternity as they relate to heaven, hell, and the afterlife in general.

Heaven and Hell

The Bible teaches that there is a place called heaven where those who have believed in Jesus as God in the flesh, the Christ, will go when their earthly bodies die. The Bible at the same time teaches that there is a place called hell or the lake of fire where those who refuse to accept Jesus as God in the flesh, the Christ, will go when their earthly bodies die. Heaven and hell are real places with locality and spatial dimensions. Since a person does not see these places, it is very difficult to picture where they are. Many believe heaven to be far, far away, up above the earth, probably due to Bible references to heaven as being upward. "If I ascend into heaven, You are there; if I make my bed in hell, behold, You are there." (Psalm 139:8). "Though they dig into hell, from there my hand shall take them; though they climb up to heaven, from there I will bring them down" (Amos 9:2). "So then, after the Lord had spoken to them, He was received up into heaven, and sat down at the right hand of God" (Mark 16:19).

Heaven being referred to as upward and hell being referred to as downward could be a result of heaven and hell being in separate dimensions—with heaven being in a higher dimension and hell in a lower dimension of some kind. If heaven is in a higher realm, it could very well be right next to people who live in a three-dimensional world. William Granville suggests that heaven might be a dimension up, the next higher spatial dimension. Therefore, it is referred to as being up or having more dimensions than three. He writes:

> **Perhaps the higher-dimensional spaces are the heavens to which we ascend at death if we have so lived on earth as to deserve such promotion... Thus at death the soul of a good man (his higher-dimensional self) shakes off the limitations of understanding, knowledge and movement which our three-dimensional space imposed on him, and enters space of four dimensions. Instead of being restricted to three degrees of freedom of motion he will then be able to move in four independent directions. Such would be his increased freedom of action that, if he could look back, his former life in our space would probably appear to him as life in a prison cell would now seem to us. Unlimited vistas of new knowledge would open up to him, and his powers of understanding and possibilities of action would have increased to an extent far beyond the present limits of human conception. Coming from the restrictions**

imposed by our space, the space of four dimensions would indeed seem heaven to him![197]

Heaven is a real place with spatial, material beings occupying it. Therefore, heaven must have a dimensional location. String theory says that more spatial dimensions do indeed exist. These presently hidden spatial dimensions are where one can find heaven. In his book, *Heaven Revealed,* Paul Enns writes about heaven being near. He says, "How would Stephen [the Acts 7 martyr] see heaven? It would be when the 'heavens opened,' indicating that heaven was not distant but nearby, in another realm. When God opens the door to heaven, people can see into heaven. *Heaven is nearby, in another realm.*"[198] Paul, writing to the Corinthians, says he knew a man who saw into heaven. Most scholars believe Paul is humbly talking about himself in this passage.

> **I know a man in Christ who fourteen years ago—whether in the body I do not know, or whether out of the body I do not know, God knows—such a one was caught up to the third heaven. And I know such a man—whether in the body or out of the body I do not know, God knows—how he was caught up into Paradise and heard inexpressible words, which it is not lawful for a man to utter (2 Corinthians 12:2-4).**

Paul received a sneak preview of the inside of heaven. Once again, heaven is closer than one might think. Heaven is in the next dimension, right next to where we reside in this three-dimensional world.

If heaven is in the next higher dimension yet undetectable to our three-dimensional senses, then heaven could very well be right next to where we presently are. When someone dies, perhaps instead of traveling far up above the earth, they travel only a millimeter away into heaven, which has been right next to them all the time. George Musser—writing about string theory, and not about the spiritual dimension at all—may be more correct about the spiritual dimension than he truly knows:

> **Is there a galaxy right next to you? It might be just an eyelash's width away, yet you can't see it, feel it, or duck over to it for some peace and calm. To get there, you'd have to travel in a fourth dimension of space, one that is perpendicular to the usual three of length, width, and height. You can't even point to it. It's all around you, everywhere and nowhere at once.**[199]

If man lives in the third dimension of space, then it is very possible that heaven or Paradise is in a higher and very near dimension of space. Paul possibly alludes to this when he says in 1 Corinthians 12 that he went to Paradise located in the third heaven. The thief on the cross went to be with Christ in Paradise that very day (Luke 23:43). Jesus said He would come and receive His disciples and take them to heaven to be with Him (John 14:1-4). Paul longed to be with Christ when he died (Philippians 1:21-23). Paul also said that when he loses his earthly body he will receive a heavenly body and will be present with the Lord (2 Corinthians 5:1-8). Heaven is located upward in the next and possibly higher dimension. Real bodies inhabit heaven, like Jesus' for example. Heaven is just beyond earth's dimensional doorway.

Hell is thought of as being downward in relation to mankind. Hell is referred to as being on the earth, and some believe it might even be in the center of the earth. The following verses illustrate this point: "Let death seize them; let them go down alive into hell, for wickedness is in their dwellings and among them" (Psalm 55:15). "I made the nations shake at the sound of its fall, when I cast it down to hell together with those who descend into the Pit; and all the trees of Eden, the choice and best of Lebanon, all that drink water, were comforted in the depths of the earth" (Ezekiel 31:16). "For if God did not spare the angels who sinned, but cast them down to hell and delivered them into chains of darkness, to be reserved for judgment" (2 Peter 2:4). All these verses refer to hell as being downward. It is a great possibility that hell is downward as a dimension. In some way going to hell is moving down as opposed to moving upward to heaven. Hell is a dimension that is away from heaven and God according to 2 Thessalonians 1:9, which says, "These shall be punished with everlasting destruction from the presence of the Lord and from the glory of His power." Hell is being separated in a dimension away from the presence of God.

A passage that illustrates the dimensionality of hell is in Luke chapter sixteen. "And being in torments in Hades, he lifted up his eyes and saw Abraham afar off, and Lazarus in his bosom" (Luke 16:23). Jesus next describes an obstacle that separates these two places. If heaven and hell are in separate dimensions, then this could be referring to the separation of the dimensions from each other. "But Abraham said, 'Son, remember that in your lifetime you received your good things, and likewise Lazarus evil things; but now he is comforted and you are tormented. And besides all this, between us and you there is a great gulf fixed, so that those who want to pass from here to you cannot, nor can those from there pass to us'" (Luke 16:25-26). The point of the story Jesus is telling us is that heaven and hell are real locations with real people inhabiting them. An impassable barrier exists between heaven and hell. The inhabitants of both places have their memory, all their senses, and bodies. Randy Alcorn, in his book entitled *Heaven*, writing about the rich man and Lazarus, says:

> **Perhaps we should consider an interpretive position that doesn't insist that every detail is literal but also recognizes that Jesus intended for us to picture people in the afterlife as real humans with thoughts and capacities (and perhaps even forms), and with the same identity, memories, and awareness from their lives and relationships on Earth. Surely Jesus intended us to envision both Heaven and Hell as real places where there are real people who came from Earth.[200]**

Hell is a real place with real locality. Hell can be found in the spiritual realm of higher or lower dimensions. It is not found in the three-dimensional world. Jesus spoke of hell several times in the Gospels. He uses the descriptive phrase "weeping and gnashing of teeth" seven times when speaking about hell. Matthew 8:11-12 says, "And I say to you that many will come from east and west, and sit down with Abraham, Isaac, and Jacob in the kingdom of heaven. But the sons of the kingdom will be cast out into outer darkness. There will be weeping and gnashing of teeth." Hell is described as a place of torment, eternal fire, but never fully dying in Mark 9:43-44: "If your hand causes you to sin, cut it off. It is better for you to enter into life maimed, rather than having two hands, to go to hell, into the fire that shall never be quenched—where 'Their worm does not die, And the fire is not quenched.'" When a person's body dies, the spirit is immediately ushered into heaven or hell. The inhabitants of both locations will have a body that houses the spirit. The locations where a dimensional body will reside for eternity are apparently in a higher or lower dimension than our present three-dimensional world.

Time and Eternity

Einstein introduced the idea of time being relative. Time and space are not as rigid as once thought; instead, they are flexible. Time was once believed to be like an inflexible yardstick that accurately measured the increments of time. After Einstein introduced relativity, time was seen as an elastic band, flexible and able to expand or contract. Calle writes about how Einstein's theory of relativity impacts time: "The faster you move, the more part of your motion through time gets converted into motion in space."[201] The faster a person moves through space, the more time slows down.

> **According to relativity, the combination of your motion through time and your motion through space equals exactly the speed of light. This combination of the three dimensions of space and the one dimension of time became what was later called spacetime, a four-dimensional entity that shows that space and time are not separate like Newton thought, but intermixed.**[202]

The speed of light is the key to understanding the flexibility of time. Calle continues on, "If you could convert all of your motion through time into motion through space, you'd be moving at the speed of light. *Time would stand still for you* [emphasis added]. This is one way of seeing why Einstein said that nothing, except light, can move at the speed of light."[203] Certainly this is merely theoretical; nothing can move at the speed of light except light itself. But can God move at the speed of light? The Bible declares that God is light. "This is the message which we have heard from Him and declare to you, that God is light and in Him is no darkness at all" (1 John 1:5). The declaration that God is light is normally seen as an analogy and illustration of God's character and characteristics—that God is "like" light in many ways. But the Bible declares that God "is" light. If God is light, then He is everywhere, and He moves at the speed of light because He is light. If God moves at the speed of light, then does time stand still for Him? Theoretically, the answer would be yes. Of course, three-dimensional beings cannot understand the full meaning of God being light and time standing still. By God being light, could that mean God has a different relationship with time than mankind does? Is moving at the speed of light or time standing still the same as living in the eternal now? The Bible indicates that God is present in the past, present, and future. Not only is God everywhere in the present, but He is also everywhere in all times, past and future. God created the dimension of time and lives outside of it. Isaiah declares that God inhabits eternity: "For thus says the High and Lofty One Who inhabits eternity, whose name is Holy, 'I dwell in the high and holy place, with him who has a contrite and humble spirit, to revive the spirit of the humble, and to revive the heart of the contrite ones'" (Isaiah 57:15). The Psalmist writes, "Before the mountains were brought forth, or ever You had formed the earth and the world, even from everlasting to everlasting, You are God" (Psalm 90:2).

A person lives in the present but has experienced the past and is moving towards the future. This is the arrow of time; it moves forward from the present to the future, allowing a person to remember the past. Eternity is usually thought of as a long, long time—time that has no end, just going on and on forever. Dr. Arthur C. Custance is a Canadian physiologist and writer who holds degrees in biblical languages and a Ph.D. in education. He writes extensively about time and eternity in his book entitled, *Journey Out of Time:*

> **Now Einstein wrestled with the problem of time, with the nature of time as opposed to eternity, of time as an abstract reality. The problem arises from the fact that one cannot have a span of time. It won't stay still long enough for us to measure it. Eternity is not time stretched to infinity on either side. There is a very significant difference between eternity and some immense stretch of time, for the simple reason that no matter how long this span of time is, we can always shorten it by chopping some off.**[204]

Dr. Custance attempts to explain that eternity is different than time by saying that if a person has an infinite number and subtracts fifty from it, they still have an infinite number; it was not shortened, because it cannot be shortened. Eternity is the quality of the experience of time in the present. For the believer, the experience will be pleasant, and awesome. For the unbeliever, without Christ, the experience will be excruciating and horrible. The believer will have no need to hope for the future; all that is ever desired is being experienced in the present. The unbeliever will be confined to the present never having hope for a better future. Both persons are present in eternity, one in heaven and the other in hell. Dr. Custance continues his writing on time:

> **Only NOW exists, and it exists as a point, not a dimension. It has only location. The past is gone, and the future is not yet. We are therefore left with nothing to shorten; only with something which has no length. Ten days never exist at one time, nor even ten seconds, nor even ten millionths of a second!... Thus, while we may speak of time which has passed, there is no such thing as eternity which has passed. Otherwise we would have to ask the absurd question, Is God older today than He was yesterday?**[205]

If time exists as a point and not a dimension, as Dr. Custance suggests, then what would happen if a dimension were added—just like having a spatial point, where there are no dimensions, merely a zero-point. Then the point is extended to make a line. The point has dimension, one dimension, back and forth on the line. If a time dimension was added to the zero-point time dimension in the spiritual dimension, what would that look like? In a zero-point spatial dimension, only the one point can be experienced. In the one-dimensional spatial dimension, the dimension that runs along the line can be experienced. In a zero-point time dimension, the present point in time can be experienced. In a one-dimensional time dimension, time can be experienced profoundly deeper. The past and future are not the focus because the fullness of the present is the focus. Time has been expanded up and down, adding dimensionality to the present time. The present is in focus in the spiritual dimension; though time does move forward, the future is not the focus and neither is the past. There are neither longings for what was, nor for what will be.

Another way of looking at the experience of time in the present three-dimensional world is the "arrow of time." In science, the arrow of time is related to entropy. Things move towards disorder in the physical universe. This is one way that a person experiences, or perceives they are experiencing, time. They see changes taking place around them. This is the result of the second law of thermodynamics. As time moves forward, things go from order to disorder.

> **In physics, the arrow in time is the direction in which entropy (disorder) increases. It's the direction of decay. ...We know exactly what time is—in fact, we are unable not to understand how it flows in our lives—but when we try to define it in precise terms, it eludes us. [Augustine] speaks of "if nothing passed away, time were not" that could, in a sense, describe how the second law of thermodynamics defines time's arrow. We know time passes because things change in a certain way as time passes.[206]**

The reason a person knows that time is moving forward is a result of entropy because they are growing older. They must input energy into life as time moves forward. The Bible says that much if not all of entropy is the result of the curse, sin, the sin-virus. Much of the description of heaven is the fact that entropy will not affect heaven and that the curse of sin has been removed. Though time moves forward, the perception of time moving forward is drastically different than life on present, sinful earth. In heaven a person does not grow old; they do not die. They don't work for food, and there is no need to maintain things. This is so foreign to mankind; it can only be read in the pages of the Bible and looked forward to in the future. We can conclude that when we no longer experience the effects of sin and entropy, we will experience eternity in its fullest.

Dr. Custance gives a final summary of eternity not being a long time but a fulfilling experience that is not bound by time:

> **Eternity, then, is not a mere extension of time. Nor is it to be confused with it. Time and eternity are clearly in different categories of experience. ...In our present life, time and eternity are somehow interdependent, though it is difficult to see what form this interdependence takes. But it is reasonably clear that we can no longer merely add stretches of time together in order to build a concept of eternity. Experience on the other side of the grave will not be "an experience of inexhaustible time" but rather an experience of timelessness.**[207]

Mankind knows no world without time, sin, and entropy. When a person arrives in the afterlife, they will no longer feel the effects of sin and entropy. Time will move forward in heaven but not in the same way it does on earth. Heaven's inhabitants will not long for the future or for the past. The present will be more than enough—an eternity in its fullest.

Is there time in heaven or not? If time is defined as a series of events or a sequence of events, then, yes, there is time in heaven. However, time is much different in heaven than on earth because of entropy. People are aging, looking towards the next event or waiting on something that is going to take place. Though heaven will have events that take place, the sense or meaning of time is no longer a factor. People will be experiencing the eternal now of life. The focus will be on the depth of experiences rather than the length.

To illustrate, consider a dream. In a person's dream, a sequence of events might happen. One might dream of standing at a living room window looking outside. Then they see another person jumping up and down on a trampoline across the street. Then, all of a sudden, the dreamer finds himself on the beach looking at the waves and hearing seagulls. A sequence of events happened in that dream. These events can be very detailed and have order. But what time was it in the dream? How much time passed in the dream? Dr. Custance writes about several studies where people were hypnotized or had dreams, and the events that took place in their minds lasted much longer than in real, earthbound time:

> **Experiments were reported in MD Canada in 1966 in which, under hypnosis, subjects could be made to experience a thousand discrete 'events' in an interval of five clock seconds. ...In another report, in one dream lasting three seconds as measured by brain wave activity, a subject imagined that 4800 seconds had passed during which time she was able to pick and count 862 [specific items].**[208]

Could heaven be similar to the time experienced in a dream? Obviously, events are happening in sequence, but the comprehension of time may not be present. An hour of events take place in only a few seconds. This emphasizes the depth of the events, not the length of the events. Time in eternity is the profound depth of the events more than the movement towards a destination. The flow of time is not the focus; the experience of the moment is the focus. There is no need for a calendar, no need for a watch.

What time is it in heaven right now? Are heaven and earth on the same time? Many people picture their loved ones who have died and gone to heaven as waiting and watching what happens on earth. Has Adam been living in heaven and waiting for four thousand years for his resurrection body? Has Paul been living in heaven and waiting for two thousand years for his resurrection body? Is a grandfather waiting for his spouse and children and grandchildren to arrive in heaven? Are heaven and earth experiencing time differently? Is time in heaven different than time on earth?

The next event where heavenly time and earthly time seem to intersect is when Christ returns to earth to receive the saints, at the rapture. At the rapture, heaven and earth appear to have events happening in both places at the same time. The Book of Revelation describes the seven years of tribulation that lead into the millennial kingdom of heaven reigning on earth. It is possible that when someone dies, they immediately experience the rapture as opposed to waiting in heaven as people arrive one by one. They quickly go to the next event that heaven and earth have in common, the rapture. About this subject, Chuck Missler writes:

> **Somebody who died 1,000 years ago and someone who died yesterday and someone who gets raptured three months from now might very well all arrive at God's throne at the same moment. One of my favorite Einstein quotes comes from a letter to the family of a friend who had passed away. He said: ...Now he has departed from this strange world a little ahead of me. That means nothing. People like us, who believe in physics, know that the distinction between past, present, and future is only a stubbornly persistent illusion.**[209]

The concept is that a believer will receive his or her glorified, resurrected body immediately upon death—with no waiting in heaven for the resurrection body.

Many scholars have grappled with the dilemma of what happens to believers when they die. The Bible says that the believer will receive his or her resurrection body when the Church is raptured. The following Scriptures state that those who die in Christ will receive their eternal body when Christ returns for the Church at the rapture.

> **Behold, I tell you a mystery: We shall not all sleep, but we shall all be changed—in a moment, in the twinkling of an eye, at the last trumpet. For the trumpet will sound, and the dead will be raised incorruptible, and we shall be changed. For this corruptible must put on incorruption, and this mortal must put on immortality. So when this corruptible has put on incorruption, and this mortal has put on immortality, then shall be brought to pass the saying that is written: "Death is swallowed up in victory" (1 Corinthians 15:51-54).**

> **For this we say to you by the word of the Lord, that we who are alive and remain until the coming of the**

> **Lord will by no means precede those who are asleep. For the Lord Himself will descend from heaven with a shout, with the voice of an archangel, and with the trumpet of God. And the dead in Christ will rise first. Then we who are alive and remain shall be caught up together with them in the clouds to meet the Lord in the air. And thus we shall always be with the Lord (1 Thessalonians 4:15-17).**

Some believe that saints who die will be only spiritual beings until the rapture. Others believe that saints who die will have temporary bodies until the rapture. Still others believe that the saints who die will experience a state similar to sleeping, called "soul sleep," until the rapture. The author of this book believes that the saints who die will find themselves immediately at the rapture along with every other saint who has passed away since Adam. Paul seems to indicate that the believer will receive his or her new body without waiting or soul sleeping. The believer will be with Christ instantaneously. The thief on the cross went to be with Jesus that very day. "And Jesus said to him, 'Assuredly, I say to you, today you will be with Me in Paradise'" (Luke 23:43). Paul wrote, "For I am hard pressed between the two, having a desire to depart and be with Christ, which is far better" (Philippians 1:23). Paul also wrote, "So we are always confident, knowing that while we are at home in the body we are absent from the Lord" (2 Corinthians 5:6). Paul indicates that the saint who dies will have a body and not live as a bodiless spirit.

> **For we know that if our earthly house, this tent, is destroyed, we have a building from God, a house not made with hands, eternal in the heavens. For in this we groan, earnestly desiring to be clothed**

> **with our habitation which is from heaven, if indeed, having been clothed, we shall not be found naked. For we who are in this tent groan, being burdened, not because we want to be unclothed, but further clothed, that mortality may be swallowed up by life (2 Corinthians 5:1-4).**

Paul indicates that when the believer dies, he is clothed with his new body. The only way this could be possible is if the time dimension in heaven is different than the time dimension on earth. In some way, unknown to mankind in this world of one-dimensional time, heavenly time is different. The drastic difference in time between heaven and earth is a possible answer to what happens when a saint dies and immediately receives a new body.

As previously stated, the rapture is the next event that must coincide with earth's three-dimensional time. Dr. Custance writes concerning this experience:

> **As each child of God passes into glory, he therefore experiences no death nor the slightest pause in consciousness, nor even any sense of departure from the loved ones who remain. For him, the time that must elapse till they too "follow" is completely absent. They depart with him. Is it any wonder that men can die joyfully in the Lord and show no sadness in "leaving their loved ones behind"?**[210]

No matter when a person dies, they immediately find themselves at the rapture being transformed with all other saints from all times past. At death, heavenly time accelerates a person forward to the rapture. Theoretically, when Adam, Abraham, Moses, David, Paul, and grandpa die, they arrive at the rapture simultaneously.

Dr. Custance continues his thought of all believers arriving at heaven together:

> **Now, this can be carried a little further. The experience of each saint is shared by all other saints, by those who have preceded and those who are to follow. For them all, all history, all intervening time between death and the Lord's return, is suddenly annihilated so that each one finds to his amazement that Adam, too, is just dying and joining him on his way to meet the Lord: and Abraham and David, Isaiah and the Beloved John, Paul and Augustine, Hudson Taylor and you and I—all in one wonderful experience meeting the Lord in a single instant together, without precedence and without the slightest consciousness of delay, none being late and none too early. ...For us who remain, this event is still future, an event greatly longed for: for those who have gone on, it has already happened—but not without us.**[211]

When believers die, they are transported to the rapture. When the rapture takes place, heavenly time and earthly time intersect, and events are happening simultaneously in all dimensions. Once the rapture takes place, earthly time and heavenly time are in sync, running parallel to each other until "the first heaven and the first earth had passed away" (Revelation 21:1). The events of the tribulation that begin after the rapture are both earthly and heavenly events. Immediately following the tribulation, the thousand-year reign of Christ is populated with both resurrected people and earthly people. This too is an intersection of heavenly and earthly time. At the end of the millennium, the Great White Throne judgment takes place right before the earth is destroyed with fire and a new heaven and new earth are created. Once the new heaven and new earth are created, earthly time is no longer.

The New Heaven and New Earth

Once the new heaven and the new earth are instituted, it appears that all of the dimensions are melded together. Revelation 21 talks about the dimensions of heaven and earth intersecting. In this chapter, the grand programmer reboots the three-dimensional earth and restarts with a new earth, having added higher dimensions. In the new earth, the spiritual dimension combines with the three-dimensional world. God, angels, and the resurrected believers will live forever in a multidimensional, fully spiritual, and fully material heaven. "Now I saw a new heaven and a new earth, for the first heaven and the first earth had passed away. Also there was no more sea. Then I, John, saw the holy city, New Jerusalem, coming down out of heaven from God, prepared as a bride adorned for her husband" (Revelation 21:1-2). The new Jerusalem that comes down from heaven to earth is both interesting and intriguing. The city that comes down appears to be a cube, though some believe it is a pyramid. However, in light of the multidimensional teachings so far, this could be a four-dimensional or multidimensional Jerusalem that comes to earth. The best three-dimensional description is a pyramid or cube-like structure.

> **And he carried me away in the Spirit to a great and high mountain, and showed me the great city, the holy Jerusalem, descending out of heaven from God, having the glory of God. Her light was like a most precious stone, like a jasper stone, clear as crystal. Also she had a great and high wall with twelve gates, and twelve angels at the gates, and names written on them, which are the names of the twelve tribes of**

the children of Israel: three gates on the east, three gates on the north, three gates on the south, and three gates on the west. Now the wall of the city had twelve foundations, and on them were the names of the twelve apostles of the Lamb. And he who talked with me had a gold reed to measure the city, its gates, and its wall. The city is laid out as a square; its length is as great as its breadth. And he measured the city with the reed: twelve thousand furlongs. Its length, breadth, and height are equal. Then he measured its wall: one hundred and forty-four cubits, according to the measure of a man, that is, of an angel (Revelation 21:10-17).

Instead of seeing the new Jerusalem as a large cube or pyramid, maybe it is a multidimensional city that John is explaining. The city is 12,000 furlongs in each direction, normally translated to be 1,400 miles. If it were a cube, it would be three-dimensional, but if it were a four-dimensional cube, it would be what is called a hypercube. A hypercube, also called a tesseract, is a four-dimensional cube (see figure 2.1). Randy Alcorn writes:

Given the dimensions of a 1,400-mile cube, if the city consisted of different levels, (we don't know this), and if each story were a generous twelve feet high, the city could have over 600,000 stories. If they were on different levels, billions of people could occupy the New Jerusalem, with many square miles per person.[212]

If the new Jerusalem were a cube, it would be big. If it were a hypercube, it would be dimensionally bigger than even Alcorn described. The cubic dimensions of the new Jerusalem have always been a bit confusing to biblical scholars. Does this city float in the air, or does it sit on the earth? Why the cube shape? If the passage is looked at from four spatial dimensions or more, then maybe the new Jerusalem is not a cube but a multidimensional city that is difficult to explain to a three-dimensional mind. A person in a resurrected body will be capable of living in four dimensions of space in heaven and in the new Jerusalem specifically.

Heaven is described in several places in the Bible. We find streets of gold (Revelation 21:21), a house with many rooms or dwelling places (John 14:2), and a river of life (Revelation 22:1). We are also told what will not be present in Heaven. "And God will wipe away every tear from their eyes; there shall be no more death, nor sorrow, nor crying. There shall be no more pain, for the former things have passed away" (Revelation 21:4). Granville writes:

> **It is evident that we as three-dimensional beings cannot have a true conception of what heaven is; being a higher space it is beyond our powers of understanding. If an accurate description of heaven were in some way available, we would not understand an iota of it, and it would be meaningless to us. ...Attempts to describe heaven always result in a description in terms of our three-dimensional environment. In this connection, it is significant to note that the Bible usually tells what heaven is not rather than what heaven is.**[213]

From the time the rapture occurs, through the tribulation and the millennial reign of Christ, until the new Jerusalem descends and the new heaven and the new earth are instituted, heaven and earth remain on the same time. Once the new Jerusalem is established events will take place, but time is no longer linked to the three-dimensional world. Eternity will be experienced in its fullest.

Chapter 12

Beam Me Up!

I am proud to be a Christian. I believe not only as a Christian but as a scientist as well. A wireless device can deliver a message through the wilderness. In prayer, the human spirit can send invisible waves to eternity, waves that achieve their goal in front of God.

–Guglielmo Marconi (1874–1937), 1909 Nobel Prize recipient in physics for his invention of the first successful system of wireless telegraphy

I believe in God, who can respond to prayers, to whom we can give trust and without whom life on this earth would be without meaning (a tale told by an idiot). I believe that God has revealed Himself to us in many ways and through many men and women and that for us here in the West the clearest revelation is through Jesus and those that have followed Him.

–Sir Nevill Mott (1905-1996), 1977 Nobel Prize recipient in physics for his research on the magnetic and electrical properties of non-crystalline semiconductors

In the year 2019, the technology of communication has revolutionized the way people communicate with each other. Calling someone who is in London from Kansas City is not only incredibly technical, it is amazingly easy and quick. Trying to imagine this technology even one-hundred years ago would have been something from a far-out science fiction book. Video calls are accomplished with simplicity from across the globe.

When calling another person from one cell phone to another, reception is vital. Cell reception or cellular coverage is the key to connecting two phones, whether by voice or video. If the phone has no reception, it won't connect to the other phone. A cell tower is essential to receiving and sending communication via wireless transmission. When wires are used for phones systems, wires are essential for the communication to go from one phone to the next. Once the connection has been established, communication can take place.

People can communicate using text, email, video, emojis, and face-to-face conversation. God communicates with people, and people can communicate with God—and the reception or connection is the key. The sacrificial death and resurrection of Jesus Christ made the reception possible. The Holy Spirit is the connection between God and mankind. A person connects to God from their three-dimensional world to the spiritual realm where God resides. Though the Bible contains hundreds of examples of people communicating with God, we find that this communication takes place through two main avenues—prayer and worship.

Prayer

Prayer is something that nearly everyone has heard of, even though its purpose and practice vary widely. Prayer is man communicating from his three-dimensional world to God in the spiritual dimension. If God is the programmer behind this digitally created universe, then does He monitor and receive communication from individuals? The Bible says yes, He does. Prayer is the opportunity for man to speak to His creator about what is on his heart and mind. This chapter is not meant to be an exhaustive study of prayer, but it is worthy of discussion here because of its cross-dimensional factors. Prayer is multidimensional communication from people to God. Hugh Ross, in his book *Beyond the Cosmos,* discusses the multidimensionality of prayer:

> **Because we are spiritual beings, we humans can pray. Through prayer we can cross the space-time manifold of the cosmos and converse with God in His extra-dimensional realm. Because prayer is extra-dimensional in its reach, it must be considered the most powerful capacity God has made available to us in our current dimensional context. Prayer is so powerful, it comes with special cautions and restrictions on its use.**[214]

Jesus Christ is the greatest example of praying to God the Father. Jesus being God, emptied himself of His godly powers when He was on earth. Though He was still one hundred percent God, He did not always have His multidimensional powers. He thus needed to communicate with God the Father as a three-dimensional man would, through prayer. The Bible records several instances where Jesus went apart to pray. "And when He had sent the multitudes away, He went up on the mountain by Himself to pray. Now when evening came, He was alone there" (Matthew 14:23). "Now in the morning, having risen a long while before daylight, He went out and departed to a solitary place; and there He prayed" (Mark 1:35). "And when He had sent them away, He departed to the mountain to pray" (Mark 6:46). "Now it came to pass in those days that He went out to the mountain to pray, and continued all night in prayer to God" (Luke 6:12). Jesus needed to pray to communicate with His father. When He prayed, He was able to enter God's presence spiritually.

Through prayer, one has access to the throne room of God, the place where God dwells and resides. Prayer is man's vehicle to access the presence of God in the spiritual realm. When Adam and Eve sinned, their access to the spiritual realm was disrupted. Mankind no longer had access to the spiritual realm, nor did they have direct access to God. Mankind's communication with God was completely blocked by their sin, but God made a way for people to access Him again through the sacrificial system. Therefore, in the Old Testament, prayer (or talking to God) usually involved a sacrifice to open the door to the spiritual realm. Since sin had disrupted the communication between God and man, an atonement for sin was required in order to open the line of communication with God once again. Abraham is a biblical example of someone who communicated with God by first building an altar and offering a sacrifice.

> **And he moved from there to the mountain east of Bethel, and he pitched his tent with Bethel on the west and Ai on the east; there he built an altar to the LORD and called on the name of the LORD (Genesis 12:8).**

> **And he went on his journey from the South as far as Bethel, to the place where his tent had been at the beginning, between Bethel and Ai, to the place of the altar which he had made there at first. And there**

Abram called on the name of the LORD (Genesis 13:3-4).

And the LORD appeared to him the same night and said, "I am the God of your father Abraham; do not fear, for I am with you. I will bless you and multiply your descendants for My servant Abraham's sake." So he built an altar there and called on the name of the LORD, and he pitched his tent there; and there Isaac's servants dug a well (Genesis 26:24-25).

Abraham built an altar to God and sacrificed an animal on it when he called upon the Lord. The sacrifice was made to gain access into the spiritual realm for communication with God. The sacrificial system was a way of approaching God throughout the Old Testament, then Christ came as the ultimate sacrifice and opened the door to God once and for all. No person can enter into the presence of God except through the cross of Christ. The writer of Hebrews says, "Let us therefore come boldly to the throne of grace, that we may obtain mercy and find grace to help in time of need" (Hebrews 4:16). Prayer is entering directly into God's presence spiritually.

In the Old Testament, the tabernacle and later the temple were physical examples of approaching God and entering His presence. God is holy and was to be approached with reverence and awe. The book of Exodus tells of the Israelites being introduced to the tabernacle where God's presence dwelt (Exodus 40:34-38). Later, when Solomon built a permanent building for the Lord, the temple, His presence dwelt among the people of Israel in Jerusalem. These are physical pictures of entering the presence of an immaterial and spiritually multidimensional God. The tabernacle and temple and their items all point to Jesus Christ. The High Priest represented the people of Israel when he entered the Holy of Holies and into the presence of God. Steven J. Cole, in a sermon from Exodus 40, says that the Jews could enter into the courtyard of the tabernacle to bring their offering or sacrifice to the altar, but that is as far as they could go. They were not allowed to enter or even look into the Holy of Holies. He says, "Only the priests could go inside the holy place, and only the high priest could enter the holy of holies once a year on the Day of Atonement. He could enter only after offering a sacrifice for his own sins and then taking the atoning blood there for the sins of the people."[215] This is a picture of the believer entering into the presence of God to communicate with Him.

In the New Testament, Christ fulfills the requirements of the Law and all the sacrificial requirements for all believers to enter God's presence. The person who trusts Christ as Savior has spiritual access to the God who created the universe. Cole states, "But when Jesus died, the way into God's presence was opened through His death. Now every believer in Christ is a priest with access, not only to the holy place, but even into the holy of holies, into God's holy presence (Hebrews 4:14-16; Ephesians 2:18; 1 Peter 2:9)!"[216] Believers of any age can spiritually enter into God's presence anytime through prayer.

The Holy Spirit intercedes on behalf of a person's spirit, connecting them to God. "Likewise the Spirit also helps in our weaknesses. For we do not know what we should pray for as we ought, but the Spirit Himself makes intercession for us with groanings which cannot be uttered. Now He who searches the hearts knows what the mind of the Spirit is, because He makes intercession for the saints according to the will of God" (Romans 8:26-27). A person is connected to the spiritual realm through the indwelling of the Holy Spirit. Prayer is more than communication from man's three-dimensional world to where God is in the spiritual realm. Prayer is spiritually entering the presence of God to communicate personally in the spiritual realm. A person can enter God's presence to praise Him, to thank Him, to hear from Him, to pray for others, and to petition God to do something in the physical realm. Tony Evans, in his book, *Victory in Spiritual Warfare,* writes this about prayer: "Simply defined, prayer is earthly permission for heavenly interference. It's earth giving heaven permission to intervene in the manifestation down here of the spiritual reality up there."[217] A person can communicate directly with God, the creator and sustainer of the universe. God can be petitioned to insert His omnipotence into the three-dimensional world and make an adjustment. The grand programmer can override the rules of the digital simulation to perform miracles and answer a believer's prayer. Prayer is multidimensional communication between a person and God. It is communicating from a three-dimensional physical world to the multidimensional spiritual realm.

Worship

Worship and prayer are very closely related. Both are built upon the sacrifice of Jesus Christ. Worship in the Old Testament was also associated with the sacrificial system, the tabernacle, and the temple. When believers enter the presence of the Lord through Jesus Christ, they can praise and worship God in the spiritual realm. Even though a person is physically limited to the three-dimensional world, spiritually they can access the spiritual realm to worship the Lord.

In the Bible, only God is intended to be a person's object of worship. The first use of the word *worship* in the New King James Version is found in Genesis 22:5: "And Abraham said to his young men, 'Stay here with the donkey; the lad and I will go yonder and worship, and we will come back to you.'" In this passage, Abraham and Isaac are going to worship the Lord. Abraham is prepared to offer a sacrifice to the Lord as he carries the wood and expresses to Isaac that God will provide the lamb.

Worship is spiritual in nature and bridges the gap between the three-dimensional and spiritual realms. John records a conversation between Jesus and the woman at the well where worship is mentioned. "But the hour is coming, and now is, when the true worshipers will worship the Father in spirit and truth; for the Father is seeking such to worship Him. God is Spirit, and those who worship Him must worship in spirit and truth" (John 4:23-24). Jesus highlights worship from a person to God as being in spirit and in truth.

When believers come to worship God, they enter God's presence spiritually. Jesus' death and resurrection provide the pathway. A person can remain in his three-dimensional world, yet spiritually transcend into the spiritual realm and experience God through worship and praise. Believers can engage in the act of worshiping God by giving, by praising through song or the spoken word, by sacrificing material possessions and personal idols, by serving, by sharing the gospel, etc. But when believers experience worship, the spirit enters the spiritual realm and communes with God—and this is much more than singing praises to the Lord in a worship service. This is the heart of the worshiper seeking to acknowledge who God is and where God deserves to be—number one in the universe. When worship happens, a spiritual encounter has taken place. Even if the worshiper neither feels nor perceives entry into the spiritual realm, it has taken place. The Holy Spirit that dwells within the believer's spirit has a trans-dimensional connection to God's throne room, and the believer has immediate access to the intimate and sacred throne room of God because of the sacrifice of Jesus Christ.

Prayer and worship are multidimensional avenues into the spiritual realm. The human race, as physical beings, are aware of their physical surroundings; but believers, as spiritual beings, are aware of the spiritual realm only through the leading and guiding of the Holy Spirit. The believers' spiritual surroundings are hidden from their physical eyes, but not from the indwelling Holy Spirit that gives them life in the spiritual realm. Prayer and worship are practical ways believers can access the spiritual realm in their personal lives.

Chapter 13

Fighting an Invisible Enemy

We have to recognize that we are spiritual beings with souls existing in a spiritual world as well as material beings with bodies and brains existing in a material world.

–Sir John Eccles (1903–1997), 1963 Nobel Prize recipient in Medicine and Physiology for establishing the relationship between inhibition of nerve cells and repolarization of a cell's membrane

The Bible is the one supreme source of revelation of the meaning of life, the nature of God and spiritual nature and need of men. It is the only guide of life, which really leads the spirit in the way of peace and salvation. There is no middle course, no neutrality. Each and every one must enlist either with the followers of Christ or those of Satan.

–Thomas Woodrow Wilson (1856–1924), twenty-eighth President of the United States, Ph.D. in politics and history, Johns Hopkins University, 1886; the only American President to have earned a Ph.D. degree to date

Conflict and war are as old as sin itself. Cain killed Abel, and people have been killing ever since. A battle exists between good and evil, between God and Satan. Though the battle initiates in the spiritual realm, it carries over into the physical realm. The United States Army has principles that guide them in times of conflict. Life or death can be determined by how well a group of men and women work together in battle. Their lives are at stake as they defend themselves and attack their enemy. The enemy seeks to kill and destroy any who would oppose or stand in their way. Victory is for the one who can attack and overcome the opposition.

For the Christian, Satan and his angels are the enemies, and they seek to kill and destroy all that follow God. The Bible gives the Christian basic principles to stand firm when attacked and to overcome the enemy by claiming the victory. The battle is spiritual in nature, yet much of the battle takes place in the physical realm. Christians must know their enemy, be prepared for battle, and stand firm when the dust settles. This chapter will focus upon the spiritual warfare that originates in the spiritual realm and impacts the person living in our three-dimensional world. This is a practical chapter that discusses how people can be attacked from the spiritual realm but also defend themselves and wage war spiritually from the three-dimensional world.

Angelic Warfare

Humans are unable to see into the spiritual realm. People have been relegated to the physical realm and their physical senses, most likely as a result of the fall and sin. Therefore, people see the results of the warfare taking place in the spiritual realm as it carries over into the physical realm. People see the ramifications of the spiritual battles in their three-dimensional world. What people see in their lives as problems, trials, temptations, attacks, or anything that opposes their faith is usually rooted in the spiritual realm. The Bible gives people a glimpse into the spiritual realm by telling of events that involve angelic warfare. Also, the Bible describes angelic warfare as it happens in various passages:

> **And when the servant of the man of God arose early and went out, there was an army, surrounding the city with horses and chariots. And his servant said to him, 'Alas, my master! What shall we do?' So he answered, 'Do not fear, for those who are with us are more than those who are with them.' And Elisha prayed, and said, 'LORD, I pray, open his eyes that he may see.' Then the LORD opened the eyes of the young man, and he saw. And behold, the mountain was full of horses and chariots of fire all around Elisha (2 Kings 6:15-17).**

In this passage, Elijah's servant is worried about the encompassing Syrian army, but Elijah could see that angels in the spiritual realm were also encompassing Elijah and his servant for protection, ready and waiting to intervene in the three-dimensional realm if needed. Elijah asked God to open his servant's eyes to enable him to see the angelic protection that Elijah fully understood was from the spiritual realm but hidden from his servant's three-dimensional view.

> **Then he said to me, "Do not fear, Daniel, for from the first day that you set your heart to understand, and to humble yourself before your God, your words were heard; and I have come because of your words. But the prince of the kingdom of Persia withstood me twenty-one days; and behold, Michael, one of the chief princes, came to help me, for I had been left alone there with the kings of Persia. Now I have come to make you understand what will happen to your people in the latter days, for the vision refers to many days yet to come" (Daniel 10:12-14).**

In this passage, an angel is sent by God as an answer to Daniel's prayers. The angel is prohibited from getting to Daniel for twenty-one days by an opposing angel identified as the Prince of Persia. Michael the archangel comes to assist the angel sent to Daniel by battling the Prince of Persia himself. Before leaving Daniel, the angel says, "Then he said, 'Do you know why I have come to you? And now I must return to fight with the prince of Persia; and when I have gone forth, indeed the prince of Greece will come. But I will tell you what is noted in the Scripture of Truth. No one upholds me against these, except Michael your prince'" (Daniel 10:20-21). Several important facts emerge from this passage concerning the spiritual realm:

1. God sends angels as ministers and messengers to the three-dimensional realm.
2. Evil angels do not want good angels ministering in the three-dimensional realm. They seek to disrupt God's ministry to people.
3. Angels fight against each other in the spiritual realm.
4. Angels residing in the spiritual realm may have powers that impact governments and nations. It is very possible that governments and high-ranking officials are heavily influenced by the spiritual realm. The possibility exists that angelic battles in the spiritual realm are mirrored in the physical realm.
5. Michael the archangel seems to be the spiritual power assigned to protect the nation of Israel.

And war broke out in heaven: Michael and his angels fought with the dragon; and the dragon and his angels fought, but they did not prevail, nor was a place found for them in heaven any longer. So the great dragon was cast out, that serpent of old, called the Devil and Satan, who deceives the whole world; he was cast to the earth, and his angels were cast out with him (Revelation 12:7-9).

In this passage, a war takes place in the spiritual realm. Michael and the good angels are battling Satan and the evil angels in the spiritual dimension.

And the armies in heaven, clothed in fine linen, white and clean, followed Him on white horses. Now out of His mouth goes a sharp sword, that with it He should strike the nations. And He Himself will rule them with a rod of iron. He Himself treads the winepress of the fierceness and wrath of Almighty God (Revelation 19:14-15).

In this passage, an angelic army comes to earth and wages war against the earthly rebels surrounding Israel. This passage describes an intersection of the spiritual and earthly realms. The angelic army, along with the redeemed saints, come into the three-dimensional realm to wipe out the armies warring against Israel.

During the ministry of Jesus, the spiritual and physical realms intersect many times in reference to demons being cast out of people. Several words are used for these spiritual beings that tormented and oppressed people:

- Evil spirit—"And that very hour He cured many of infirmities, afflictions, and evil spirits; and to many blind He gave sight" (Luke 7:21).

- Unclean spirit—"And when He had called His twelve disciples to Him, He gave them power over unclean spirits, to cast them out, and to heal all kinds of sickness and all kinds of disease" (Matthew 10:1).
- Demon (devil in the KJV)—"So the demons begged Him, saying, 'If You cast us out, permit us to go away into the herd of swine'" (Matthew 8:31). "So the devils besought him, saying, If thou cast us out, suffer us to go away into the herd of swine" (Matthew 8:31 KJV).

Matthew, Mark, and Luke all record encounters with demons during Jesus' ministry, though John does not record any such encounters. The only time the word *demon* is used in the gospel of John is when the Pharisees accuse Jesus of having a demon (John 7:20; 8:48-52; 10:20-21).

During His earthly ministry, Jesus displayed power over the spiritual realm by commanding evil spirits to be cast out of people. Much is not understood about evil spiritual beings occupying and controlling a person's physical body, but an undeniable intersection of the spiritual and physical realms takes place during these events. Jesus, being completely in tune with the spiritual realm, could identify and remove these demons. Demons that somehow controlled and oppressed a person's body displayed physical evidences in people—producing seizures (Matthew 17:14-17), causing muteness (Matthew 9:32-33), giving super-human strength (Mark 5:2-4), and giving either psychic abilities or the counterfeit of such abilities (Acts 16:16-18).

Angelic warfare in the spiritual realm is real. Most people are unaware of the battles taking place and the impact that the spiritual realm has on the three-dimensional realm. How does warfare in the spiritual realm impact the believer in daily life? What does this warfare in the spiritual realm look like to the person living in the physical realm?

The Reality of the Spiritual Realm as Related to the Believer

The spiritual realm is alluded to all throughout the Old and New Testaments. Several times it is explicitly mentioned, especially by Paul in the book of Ephesians as he wrote about the powers that reside in the spiritual realm. In Ephesians 1:3, Paul writes, "Blessed be the God and Father of our Lord Jesus Christ, who has blessed us with all spiritual blessings in heavenly places in Christ." The Greek word that is translated *heavenly places* is *epouranios*.[218] This Greek word is used twenty times in the New Testament, and five of those times were by Paul in the book of Ephesians. In each instance that *epouranios* is used in Ephesians, it is speaking of the spiritual realm. In Ephesians 1:3, Paul is making a point that the believer has already been given every spiritual blessing. Through the death, burial, and resurrection of Jesus Christ, the believer has already won the spiritual victory. The "heavenly places" spoken of by Paul in this verse is the spiritual dimension.

Paul speaks of the spiritual realm again in Ephesians 1:20: "Which He worked in Christ when He raised Him from the dead and seated Him at His right hand in the heavenly places." Here Paul is stating that Christ is presently in the spiritual dimension or realm. In the next chapter, Paul writes, "And raised us up together, and made us sit together in the heavenly places in Christ Jesus" (Ephesians 2:6). Paul makes a bold and cross-dimensional statement in this verse. He claims that the believer is both in the three-dimensional physical world and in the higher-dimensional spiritual realm at the same time. Tony Evans, writing about this verse, says, "Right this very minute, you and I are spiritually seated with Christ in the spiritual realm. ...Where you are physically is not the only place you are located. You are equally located in another realm."[219] This verse makes so much more sense when the spiritual dimension is understood. Many commentators will only go so far as to say this verse is speaking of a believer being positionally in the spiritual realm—the believer is only theoretically there and will be fully in the spiritual realm when they die. Taken from the spiritual dimension perspective, Tony Evans seems to be correct when he says that Paul is stating that believers are spiritually in the spiritual realm with Christ once they are saved.

Paul writes about the spiritual realm again in the next chapter: "To the intent that now the manifold wisdom of God might be made known by the church to the principalities and powers in the heavenly places" (Ephesians 3:10). Here Paul describes the dark and demonic forces in the spiritual dimension as principalities and powers. This real dimension of space where angels, both good and evil, reside and what happens in this realm impacts the three-dimensional world. Paul understood demonic attack from the spiritual realm would affect him in the physical, three-dimensional realm. Evans writes, "Physical solutions cannot fix physical problems that originate in the spiritual realm."[220] The attacks by Satan and his demons in the three-dimensional realm is spiritual warfare. Attacking the physical elements of that physical problem will never fix it since the problem originates in the spiritual realm. Evans continues, "If all you see is what you see, you will never see all that there is to be seen."[221] When a person never sees that their problem is spiritual, then they will never see the real root of the problem.

In Ephesians 6, Paul elaborates more on the spiritual realm and its constituents. "For we do not wrestle against flesh and blood, but against principalities, against powers, against the rulers of the darkness of this age, against spiritual hosts of wickedness in the heavenly places" (Ephesians 6:12). Paul is clearly talking about the spiritual realm and the demonic forces and beings that work there. The Greek word translated *heavenly places* is the same Greek word that was translated *heavenly places* in the previous four verses where the word is found. The King James translators used *high places* in Ephesians 6:12 to perhaps delineate between the heavenly dimension where Christ is and the dimension where Satan and his demons are located. Since it is the same Greek word, it is probable that it is the very same dimension, the spiritual realm. It might also be different dimensions or locations within the spiritual realm. What is clear is that the spiritual realm is where angelic beings and God are located. Also, it is apparently where believers are located spiritually, even though they are physically on earth at the same time.

Paul, writing to the Corinthians, refers to the spiritual realm and its impact on a person. "For though we walk in the flesh, we do not war according to the flesh. For the weapons of our warfare are not carnal but mighty in God for pulling down strongholds" (2 Corinthians 10:3-4). Paul stresses that the battle originates in the spiritual realm, and it influences the physical realm. Even though a person sees the physical results of the battle, it is a spiritual war.

The Battlefield for Spiritual Warfare Is the Mind

Many verses in the New Testament show that there is a definite struggle between Satan and God over people's minds and thoughts. The battlefield where spiritual warfare takes place is in the mind, thoughts, or a person's consciousness. Satan seeks to impact a person's thinking and beliefs. What a person sees, feels, hears, or interprets with their five senses impacts their thoughts and beliefs. What a person thinks and believes impacts their physical and spiritual life.

Satan and his demons desire to influence and control a person's thinking. Several verses support this truth. Satan blinds unbelievers' minds or thoughts from seeing the truth. "Whose minds the god of this age has blinded, who do not believe, lest the light of the gospel of the glory of Christ, who is the image of God, should shine on them" (2 Corinthians

4:4). Paul writing to the church at Ephesus says, "This I say, therefore, and testify in the Lord, that you should no longer walk as the rest of the Gentiles walk, in the futility of their mind, having their understanding darkened, being alienated from the life of God, because of the ignorance that is in them, because of the blindness of their heart" (Ephesians 4:17-18). In this passage Paul uses several words that emphasize a person's thinking or thoughts. He uses the words *mind, understanding,* and *ignorance.* To the Corinthians, Paul writes, "But I fear, lest somehow, as the serpent deceived Eve by his craftiness, so your minds may be corrupted from the simplicity that is in Christ" (2 Corinthians 11:3). Paul warns the church that their minds are susceptible to being deceived by Satan and his angelic workers. Paul also writes, "Lest Satan should take advantage of us; for we are not ignorant of his devices" (2 Corinthians 2:11). Here the word translated *devices* is the same word translated *minds* in 2 Corinthians 3:14, 4:4, 11:3; Philippians 4:7 and *thought* in 2 Corinthians 10:5.[222] *Minds* and *devices* being the same Greek word, speaks of purposes, intentions, plans, or strategy. What is Satan's strategy? To deceive people, to blind people from knowing and doing God's will. Satan desires to blind the unbeliever to the saving knowledge of Jesus Christ. Satan desires to deceive the believer from the knowledge and truth that leads to obedience, growth, and maturity.

Paul explains the battle of a believer's thought life in 2 Corinthians 10:3-5: "For though we walk in the flesh, we do not war according to the flesh. For the weapons of our warfare are not carnal but mighty in God for pulling down strongholds, casting down arguments and every high thing that exalts itself against the knowledge of God, bringing every thought into captivity to the obedience of Christ." The Greek word translated *thought* in verse five is *noema.*[223] This word is found six times in the New Testament, with five of them being found in 2 Corinthians and the other in Philippians. The Greek word refers to a person's thoughts or thinking. In this passage, Paul explicitly declares that a person's struggle is found in the spiritual realm, and he gives three actions to be taken by the believer.

First, they are to "pull down" strongholds. Some believers see these as angels that have exerted some kind of power over a person or group of people. However, the context of the passage, taken with the next two actions, point to the pulling down of strongholds as being mental strongholds, strongholds of unbelief, or strongholds of sin in a person's life. Rick Warren says this about tearing down strongholds:

> **The apostle Paul says here that our job in this battle is to "destroy strongholds." You know what a stronghold is? It is a mental block. Paul is talking about pretentions, arguments set up against the knowledge of God. This is a mental battle. And he says, "Destroy these strongholds." A stronghold can be one of two things:**
>
> - **It can be a worldview, such as materialism, hedonism, Darwinism, secularism, relativism, communism, atheism. All of the different *-isms* are mental strongholds that people set up against the knowledge of God.**

- **A stronghold can also be a personal attitude. Worry can be a stronghold. Seeking the approval of other people can be a stronghold. Anything that you turn into an idol in your life can be a stronghold—fear, guilt, resentment, insecurity. All of these things can be strongholds in your mind. And the Bible says that we are to tear them down.[224]**

Secondly, the believer is to "cast down" imaginations and high things that exalt themselves against God. This is clearly an action to be taken against thoughts that are directly contrary to the truth or knowledge of God. Any thought or belief that disagrees or is in direct opposition to the truth of God is to be cast down.

The third action to be taken by the believer is "bringing into captivity" every thought and aligning it with Christ. This is taking thoughts that are contrary to the truth and locking them up or making them prisoner. The opposing thoughts are to be changed and conformed into Christ-like thoughts.

Since the battle is in the mind and thoughts of each individual, deception seems to be the number one tactic by the enemy in spiritual warfare. Satan uses entryways to influence a person's thoughts or mind. When a person's mind or thoughts have been impacted or affected in some way by their experiences, Satan has an entry point. Examples could be practicing or experimenting in the occult, taking drugs, past sins, various kinds of abuse, or trauma. Satan will use these gateways to wage war against the believer. He seeks to deceive the unbeliever into remaining focused on the physical world only and not believing the truth of Scripture. Satan seeks to deceive the believer into remaining spiritually immature and not growing in the spiritual truth of Scripture. A part of spiritual warfare is aligning one's thoughts with God's Word and believing spiritual truth even if it appears to contradict the physical world. A part of spiritual warfare is not remaining immature or carnal, but growing in the Word of God. The word *carnal* is used in the Bible to refer to a person who is focused on the physical only and not the spiritual. Paul speaking to the church at Rome, says, "For to be carnally minded is death, but to be spiritually minded is life and peace. Because the carnal mind is enmity against God; for it is not subject to the law of God, nor indeed can be" (Romans 8:6-7).

Can Satan or a demon enter a person's mind? This is a difficult question, and answers differ. A person's consciousness is connected to the spiritual realm in some manner. The person's soul, mind, emotions, will, and consciousness intersect the spiritual realm in some way. Satan may have influence into a person's mind as it intersects the spiritual realm. Rather than Satan or a demon being able to enter a believer's mind or being able to whisper into a believer's mind, it seems more likely that Satan and his demons influence the things that sway a person's mind or thoughts. People, because of their sin, have been relegated to the physical, three-dimensional world. Satan and his demons seek to use the five senses to impact the person's thoughts, and thus a battle is waged.

The believer has already been seated with Christ in the spiritual realm (Ephesians 2:6). The victory has already been won in the end. Satan has already lost the war. Evans writes,

"Any advancement they [Satan and his demons] make in your life or on this earth is because they have been given permission to do so. The only power they have is the power that is granted to them."[225] Satan and his workers of iniquity have no authority in a believer's life unless they have been granted permission. This could be called a gateway or entrance for Satan and his demons—one that has been allowed by the believer. These gateways are areas where people willfully turn from truth and follow the flesh or the world. Believers who allow drugs or emotions or fleshly desires to control them are willfully allowing Satan and his demons entrance into their lives. Believers allowing themselves to be controlled by worldly doctrine, past sins, trauma, emotional pain—anything that gives Satan an entry—will result in Satan and his demons having the ability to deceive those people.

Waging War from the Three-dimensional World

The Bible teaches that Satan and his demons are attacking and influencing believers' thoughts and minds. Therefore, the Bible equally directs believers' thoughts and minds as a way of combatting satanic attacks. Romans 12:2 says, "And do not be conformed to this world, but be transformed by the renewing of your mind, that you may prove what is that good and acceptable and perfect will of God." Paul is teaching that believers are to renew their minds and thoughts by conforming to God's truth. This is believing and acting on truth in one's life. When believers conform their minds to believe and live truth, spiritual warfare is waged in the spiritual realm. Paul again writes, "Do not lie to one another, since you have put off the old man with his deeds, and have put on the new man who is renewed in knowledge according to the image of Him who created him" (Colossians 3:9-10). Paul speaks of the believer being "renewed" in the knowledge of God. The believer is to learn and apply truth in the three-dimensional realm in order to impact the believer's consciousness in the spiritual realm. Studying the truth of the Scriptures not only firms up the foundation of a person's belief and faith, but it also counters false doctrine. Knowing and applying the truth of God's Word is the key act of spiritual warfare for the believer. The New Testament emphasizes the protection of the believer's mind and thoughts by being vigilant (1 Peter 5:8) and alert (1 Thessalonians 5:8; 1 Peter 4:7).

The believer's thoughts and mind are of the utmost importance and foundational in spiritual warfare. In the book of Acts, when Paul goes to Ephesus to evangelize and start a church, he encounters a city that is under the control of the spiritual realm. Paul did many miracles there, and he cast out evil spirits from people (Acts 19:12). The passage also describes some unbelieving Jews that attempt to cast an evil spirit out of a person in the name of Jesus. The evil spirit attacks them, and they flee from the house naked and wounded (Acts 19:14-16). Many people in Ephesus believed in Jesus as the Christ, and they burned their occultic and dark magic books. "Also, many of those who had practiced magic brought their books together and burned them in the sight of all. And they counted up the value of them, and it totaled fifty thousand pieces of silver" (Acts. 19:19). The background of how Paul came into Ephesus and the evil that was over the city gives a perfect backdrop to the letter he later writes to the church. He writes of the spiritual realm and gives guidance for protection against Satan and his demons. In Ephesians 6:13-17, Paul explains the spiritual armor the believer must possess when waging spiritual warfare.

> **Therefore take up the whole armor of God, that you may be able to withstand in the evil day, and having done all, to stand. Stand therefore, having girded your waist with truth, having put on the breastplate of righteousness, and having shod your feet with the preparation of the gospel of peace; above all, taking the shield of faith with which you will be able to quench all the fiery darts of the wicked one. And take the helmet of salvation, and the sword of the Spirit, which is the word of God.**

Truth

The first piece of spiritual armor Paul mentions is the belt of truth. The foundation piece that holds all the other pieces into place is truth. The believer can access the spiritual realm and do battle using truth. Satan's tactic is to deceive and lie. The Bible says, "You are of your father the devil, and the desires of your father you want to do. He was a murderer from the beginning, and does not stand in the truth, because there is no truth in him. When he speaks a lie, he speaks from his own resources, for he is a liar and the father of it" (John 8:44).

To combat against the lies and deceit, the believer must know and believe the truth. Truth is what holds all the armor and weapons together. The mental imagery is that the believer must have a firm understanding and be wrapped with truth. The Word of God gives a person the truth to believe and trust. As believers look at themselves, their situation, and the world around them, everything must be interpreted and seen in light of the truth of God's Word. If people feel or see themselves as worthless, what is the truth? In Christ, all people are eternal and priceless. If people turn to drugs or alcohol for an escape or relief, they do not see the truth. If people feel unloved, the truth is that God loves them. Satan attacks with lies, while truth counters the lies. Evans writes:

> **When you wear the belt of truth and operate with it by aligning your mind, will, and emotions underneath God's view on a matter—His truth—He will then empower you to fight your spiritual battles with freedom of greater mobility and increased stability. By knowing and functioning according to the truth of God, you will be on your way to experiencing victory over anything or anyone seeking to overcome or defeat you.**[226]

Righteousness

The next piece of armor mentioned by Paul is the breastplate of righteousness. The breastplate protected the heart. Paul is commanding the Ephesians to place the righteousness of God over their hearts for protection in spiritual warfare. Satan seeks to do damage to the mind, will, and emotions of the believer. It is imperative for believers to take precautions and protect their hearts from the lies and deceit of the devil. Jesus' righteousness, even though it is applied to believers from the spiritual realm, is the ultimate protection against spiritual attack. A believer's own righteousness is unable to protect him—in fact, according to the Bible, it is like filthy rags (Isaiah 64:6). It is not only insufficient, but it also does not protect the heart. The righteousness of Christ is the believer's righteousness after salvation. Believers have protection in the spiritual realm due to Jesus' righteousness and must have faith that God will use it to protect them.

Peace

Believers are to be shod with the gospel of peace, which is what the believer proclaims to get through the trials and tribulations of life. Believers can have a peace that only God can give, through Jesus Christ. This peace gives believers the faith that God is in control and that all things will work according to His plan, even though everything is in chaos at the moment. Trusting in the world and the way of mankind never brings peace. Believers shod with this gospel of peace can have trust in God as the provider of salvation and a way of living forever in heaven through Christ. Evans elaborates on these shoes:

> **Every attack on peace in your life needs to be taken straight back to the spiritual realm and replaced with what God has to say on the matter. When you do that, you will wear shoes unlike many others'. You will wear shoes that let the demonic realm, yourself, and others know that you are covered by God's armor. You will walk without becoming weary, and in those shoes you will find the calming power of peace.**[227]

Faith

The believer's faith in the truth of God's Word is of utmost importance in extinguishing the satanic attacks that originate in the spiritual realm. Warren Wiersbe writes:

> **In Paul's day, arrows, dipped in some flammable substance and ignited, were shot at the enemy. Satan shoots "fiery darts" at our hearts and minds: lies, blasphemous thoughts, hateful thoughts about others, doubts, and burning desires for sin. If we do not by faith quench these darts, they will light a fire within, and we will disobey God. We never know when Satan will shoot a dart at us, so we must always walk by faith and use the shield of faith.**[228]

Faith is believing God is telling the truth. Faith is taking God at His word. It is by faith that believers enact the truth of God's Word to work on their behalf.

Salvation

The helmet of salvation protects the head from blows that Satan and his demons throw at the believer. The believer's salvation is the helmet that protects and gives confidence in the battle. John MacArthur writes:

> **The fact that the helmet is related to salvation indicates that Satan's blows are directed at the believer's security and assurance in Christ. The two dangerous edges of Satan's spiritual broadsword are discouragement and doubt. To discourage us he points to our failures, our sins, our unresolved problems, our poor health, or to whatever else seems negative in our lives in order to make us lose confidence in the love and care of our heavenly Father.**[229]

Since the battle is in the mind and spiritual realm, the believer's assurance of salvation protects the mind from being wounded. A person's salvation is the bedrock for experiencing all the fullness of the Christian life. A failure to realize and stand firm on Christ's finished work in the believer's heart and life means giving in and losing the spiritual battle.

The Word of God

Paul draws an analogy between a sword and the Word of God. The Word of God is a spiritual sword that is used in the spiritual realm. The Bible is the supernatural communication of God to all people in the physical realm. The truth contained in the Word of God is the believer's weapon to reach into the spiritual realm and do battle. MacArthur writes, "The word of God is so powerful that it transforms men from the realm of falsehood to that of truth, from the realm of darkness to that of light, and from the realm of sin and death to that of righteousness and life. It changes sadness into joy, despair into hope, stagnation into growth, childishness into maturity, and failure into success."[230] The Word of God is where the power lies for the believer doing battle in the spiritual realm. The Word is truth and the believer is defenseless and powerless without it. MacArthur continues, "Every time God's Word is used to lead a person to salvation, it gives witness to its power to cut a swath through Satan's dominion of darkness and bring the light of life to a lost soul."[231]

Conclusion

A spiritual realm exists beyond the physical realm. The spiritual realm or higher dimension is where one finds genuine reality. When a believer understands that the spiritual realm is a real place with locality and dimensionality, it helps him understand the Bible in a deeper and fuller way. God, as the grand programmer, becomes immeasurably infinite, yet purposeful and more personal. Heaven becomes more tangible and real, not mystic and vague. Angels become more than invisible spirits floating around in the physical realm. The spiritual realm becomes very real. The truth is, the spiritual realm is more real than the digitally interpreted physical realm.

Everything in the physical world is made up of miniscule packets of energy. What people see as their reality is the interpretation of the energetic building blocks called atoms that make up all matter. Atoms, and consequently all substances, including people are mostly empty space. The physical, three-dimensional world is digital. A person uses his sensory receptors to see, touch, hear, taste, and smell. A person's world is only as real as the interpretation of the data by the physical senses. People are also spiritual beings. But they have been confined in the physical realm of their five senses as a result of sin. The sin-virus entered the physical realm through Adam and Eve causing their spiritual senses to be broken. As a result of the sin-virus entering the world, everyone born to Adam and Eve is born spiritually dead. God Himself entered the program as Jesus to remedy the sin-virus problem.

Though people lost their ability to see into the spiritual realm, God left clues to His multidimensional existence in the physical realm. God is a spiritual being living primarily outside of man's three-dimensional realm. His characteristics and attributes always describe Him so that three-dimensional man can attempt to understand Him. God is the grand programmer and communicates with mankind through the Bible, Jesus, and the Holy Spirit. God gave people the Bible as a guide to who He is and who they are, as well as how to live effectively in the broken three-dimensional world.

The closer science moves towards the fundamental elements of an atom, the weirder the results, and the stranger the theories. String theory says a mathematical possibility exists for more spatial dimensions making up the universe than the three presently known. Science has also discovered that time is more flexible and less predictable than it was once believed to be. The person living in the three-dimensional realm cannot fully understand an additional higher dimension. Using geometry, a person can grasp how a two-dimensional being attempts to understand a three-dimensional world. This helps the three-dimensional being in the attempt to understand a four-dimensional or higher-dimensional world. Recent discoveries in science actually point to a creator. Science and the Bible both point to something beyond the physical dimension, a spiritual realm.

When a person can understand that the spiritual realm is another dimension of space where angelic beings live and where heaven is located, their understanding of the Bible is further enlightened and expanded. It is very possible that angels enter the physical realm from the adjacent spiritual realm. Heaven appears to be closer than one thinks, and angels could be only an eyelash width away. When believers die, we may move less than a millimeter into heaven. The unseen, spiritual realm is accessible to a person only through the Holy Spirit, death, or the rapture. The believer accesses the spiritual realm through the Holy Spirit using spiritual eyes. Paul wrote to the church at Corinth about the earthly body and the heavenly body that the believer will receive in heaven. Paul says that the believer walks by faith and not by sight (2 Corinthians 5:6-7). The only way for the believer to see the spiritual realm is by faith, by understanding and trusting in the truth that the grand programmer has given to them. The eyes of faith can see truth even though it may not make sense. It is like trusting the numbers or trusting the figures to be correct. Just like a scientist trusts the formula, or trusts the equation, a believer trusts the truth of God's Word.

When a believer understands the spiritual dimension, he has a deeper understanding of God and how He operates with mankind. He richly understands prayer and worship. Also, the believer can understand a deeper reality of heaven and hell and have a more complete view of angels, both good and evil. He knows there is more to the universe than the three dimensions of space and one dimension of time that humans experience—and definitely more to life than what meets the eye...the physical eye, that is!

Where will you spend eternity when you die?

If you were to die today, do you know where you would spend eternity? Heaven or hell? The Bible makes it clear that man has sinned and that sin separates us from God. If we die in our sins, we cannot enter into heaven. We cannot take even one sin into heaven or it will ruin the perfect paradise. The question for us is, how do I get rid of my sins so that I may enter into heaven sinless? Good works, money, or attending services in a religious building will never erase our sins. Instead, our sins must be paid for...our sins must be forgiven.

Jesus Christ was God in the flesh. He came to earth and lived a perfect life, died on the cross for the sins of the world, and rose again in victory over sin and death. Because of his substitutionary death on the cross, Jesus has the authority to forgive us of our sins so that we can be considered sinless and spend eternity in heaven. Jesus' forgiveness is free to those who come to God and acknowledge their sinfulness, repent or turn from their life of unbelief, and ask for forgiveness. The following is a guide to help you if you desire to receive this forgiveness.

How can I know I will go to heaven?

1. **Realize God loves you!**

   "For God so loved the world that He gave His only begotten Son. That whoever believes in Him should not perish but have everlasting life." (John 3:16)

2. **Because of our sin, we are separated from God.**

   "For all have sinned and fall short of the glory of God." (Romans 3:23)

3. **The penalty for our sin is death.**

   "For the wages of sin is death..." (Romans 6:23)

4. **Jesus died in our place.**

   "But God demonstrates His own love toward us, in that while we were sinners, Christ died for us." (Romans 5:8)

5. **Salvation is a gift to be accepted.**

   "...but the gift of God is eternal life in Christ Jesus our Lord." (Romans 6:23)

   "...believe on the Lord Jesus Christ, and you will be saved..." (Acts 16:31)

   "If you confess with your mouth the Lord Jesus and believe in your heart that God raised Him from the dead, you will be saved." (Romans 10:9)

6. **If you would like to receive God's gift of salvation, tell Him.**

   Dear God, I am a sinner in need of salvation. I believe in Jesus as my Savior and Lord. Please forgive me of my sins. Thank you for saving me. Amen.

Congratulations! Jesus is your Savior. When you die, you will go to heaven because of what Jesus has done for you!

"For whoever calls on the name of the Lord shall be saved." (Romans 10:13)

Notes

Introduction

1 "Stories of Joplin: The Spook Light," Joplin Missouri Official Website, https://www.joplinmo.org /575/The-Spook-Light (accessed November 10, 2019).

2 Ibid.

3 Ibid.

4 Michael S. Heiser, *Supernatural* (Bellingham, WA: Lexham Press, 2015), 17.

5 Mike Mariani, "American Exorcism," The Atlantic, December 2018, https://www.theatlantic .com/magazine/archive/2018/12/catholic-exorcisms-on-the-rise/573943/ (accessed May 24, 2019).

6 Ibid.

7 Emma Green, "A Lot of Americans Think the Spirit World Exists," The Atlantic, May 7, 2014, https://www.theatlantic.com/national/archive/2014/05/have-you-been-possessed-by-spirits/361680/ (accessed May 24, 2019).

8 Bernard Haisch, *The God Theory: Universes, Zero-Point Fields and What's Behind It All* (San Francisco, CA: Weiser Books, 2006), 24-25.

Chapter 1: The Paranormal, the Supernatural, and the Bible

9 "Merriam-Webster Dictionary," Merriam-Webster, https://www.merriam-webster.com/ dictionary/paranormal (accessed September 28, 2019).

10 Owen Edwards, "How Thomas Jefferson Created His Own Bible," Smithsonian.com, https://www.smithsonianmag.com/arts-culture/how-thomas-jefferson-created-his-own-bible-5659505/ (accessed May 25, 2019).

11 Ibid.

12 Walter C. Kaiser, *Hard Sayings of the Bible* (Downers Grove, IL: InterVarsity Press, 1996), 80, WORDsearch CROSS e-book.

13 *The Holy Bible: New King James Version* (NKJV). Nashville: Thomas Nelson, 1982. All subsequent Scripture quotations are taken from the NKJV unless otherwise noted.

14 James Strong, *Strong's Talking Greek and Hebrew Dictionary* (Austin, TX: WORDsearch Corp., 2007), under "G166," WORDsearch CROSS e-book.

15 Ibid., under "G5550".

16 Hugh Ross, *Beyond the Cosmos: The Extra-Dimensionality of God,* 2nd ed. (Colorado Springs, CO: NavPress, 1999), 54.

17 Ken Ham, "What Was God Doing Before Creation?" October 2, 2012. Answers in Genesis, https://answersingenesis.org/answers/biblical-authority-devotional/where-does-god-live/what-was-god-doing-before-creation/ (accessed May 27, 2019).

18 Kenneth O. Gangel and Stephen J. Bramer, *Holman Old Testament Commentary – Genesis,* ed. Max Anders (Nashville, TN: Broadman & Holman, 2003), 153, WORDsearch CROSS e-book.

19 Ross, 57.

20 Arthur Willink, *The World of the Unseen* (London: MacMillan and Co., 1893), 162-63.

21 Chuck Missler, *Beyond Time and Space* (Coeur d'Alene, ID: Koinonia House, 2016), 568, Kindle Edition.

Chapter 2: Step into the Next Dimension

22 Chris McMullen Ph.D., *The Visual Guide to Extra Dimensions* (n.p.: Custom Books, 2008), 1:11.

23 Ibid., 12.

24 Ibid.

25 William Anthony Granville, *The Fourth Dimension and the Bible* (Boston: The Gotham Press, 1922), 15.

26 Rudy v. B. Rucker, *Geometry, Relativity, and the Fourth Dimension* (New York: Dover Publications, 1977), 1.

27 Missler, *Beyond Time and Space*, 323, Kindle Edition.

28 Granville, 20.

29 Edwin A. Abbott, *Flatland: A Romance of Many Dimensions* (Mineola, NY: Dover Publications, 1992), 1.

30 Ibid., 55-62.

31 Ibid., 77-81.

32 Ibid., 81-82.

Chapter 3: Time Machines and Twilight Zones

33 Carlos I. Calle, *Einstein for Dummies* (Hoboken, NJ: Wiley Publishing, 2005), 114.

34 Ibid., 116.

35 Ibid., 65.

36 Andrew Zimmerman Jones and Daniel Robbins, *String*

Theory for Dummies (Hoboken, NJ: Wiley Publishers, 2010), 26.

37 Ibid., 27.

38 Calle, 67.

39 Jones and Robbins, 84

40 Calle, 145.

41 Jones and Robbins, 96.

42 Ibid., 97.

43 Ibid., 98.

44 Lambert Dolphin, "The History of Hyperspace," Koinonia House, http://www.khouse.org/articles/1997/29/ (accessed June 5, 2019).

45 Paul Halpern, *The Great Beyond: Higher Dimensions, Parallel Universes and the Extraordinary Search for a Theory of Everything* (Hoboken, NJ: J. Wiley, 2004), 18.

46 Paul Halpern, "Spiritual Hyperplane: How Spiritualists of the 19th Century Forged a Lasting Association between Higher Dimensions and the Occult World," Aeon, https://aeon.co/essays/the-occult-roots-of-higher-dimensional-research-in-physics (accessed June 5, 2019).

47 Barry Bradford, "Houdini's Greatest Trick – Debunking Fake Psychics," BarryBradford.com, http://barrybradford.com/houdini-greatest-trick/ (accessed June 6, 2019).

48 Ibid.

Chapter 4: Blown Minds and String Theory

49 Chuck Missler, *Beyond Newton* (Coeur d'Alene, ID: Koinonia House, 2016), 714, Kindle Edition.

50 Jones and Robbins, 26.

51 Ibid., 120.

52 Meghan Rock, *String Theory*, Great Discoveries in Science (New York: Cavendish Square Publishing, 2017), under "Introduction: Quantum Mechanics," https://www.hoopladigital.com/ play/12171869 (accessed June 14, 2019).

53 Ibid., under "Chapter 2: The Structure of Atoms".

54 Missler, *Beyond Newton*,107, Kindle Edition.

55 Missler, *Beyond Time & Space*, 426, Kindle Edition.

56 Ibid.

57 Kelly Izlar, "Atomic Flashback: A Century of the Bohr Model," CERN, https://home.cern/ news/news/physics/ atomic-flashback-century-bohr-model (accessed October 13, 2019).

58 Joseph Selbie, *The Physics of God: Unifying Quantum Physics, Consciousness, M-Theory, Heaven, Neuroscience, and Transcendence* (Wayne, NJ: New Page Books/Career Press, 2018), 59.

59 Jones and Robbins, 100.

60 Ibid., 102.

61 Ibid., 105.

62 Chuck Missler, *Beyond Perception* (Coeur d'Alene, ID: Koinonia House, 2016), 403, Kindle Edition.

63 Selbie, 28-29.

64 Ibid., 29.

65 Ibid., 33.

66 Dennis Zetting, *A Quantum Case for God* (Lynden, WA: Quantum Creation Ministries, 2016), 37.

67 Ibid., 58.

68 Missler, *Beyond Perception*, 409, Kindle Edition.

69 Ibid., 430, Kindle Edition.

70 Selbie, 89.

71 Ibid., 94.

72 Rock, *String Theory*, under "Chapter 4: What is String Theory?" e-book.

73 Jones and Robbins,14.

74 George Musser, *The Complete Idiot's Guide to String Theory* (New York: Alpha, 2008), 172.

75 Ibid.

76 Jones and Robbins, 15-16.

77 Haisch, 36.

78 Missler, *Beyond Newton*, 765, Kindle Edition.

79 Nola Taylor Redd, "What Is Dark Matter?" Space.com, https://www.space.com/20930-dark-matter.html (accessed August 13, 2019).

80 Missler, *Beyond Perception*, 819, Kindle Edition.

81 Coby Bartolucci, "Dark Matter or Heavenly Matter?" The Odyssey Online, March 1, 2016, https://www.theodysseyonline.com/heavenly-matter-theory (accessed August 13, 2019).

82 Missler, Beyond Perception, 816, Kindle Edition.

83 Jones and Robbins, 114.

84 Ibid., 114-115.

85 Ibid., 261.

86 Zetting, 154.

Chapter 5: Living in a Designer World

87 Haisch, 37.

88 Selbie, 181.

89 Benjamin Wormald, "Scientists and Belief," Pew Research Center, https://www.pewforum.org/2009/11/05/scientists-and-belief/ (accessed June 11, 2019).

90 www.ASA3.org

91 Amir D. Aczel, "Why Science Does Not Disprove God," Time, April 27, 2014, https://time.com/77676/why-science-does-not-disprove-god/ (accessed June 12, 2019).

92 Haisch, 131.

93 P. C. W. Davies, *The Mind of God: The Scientific Basis for a Rational World* (New York: Simon & Schuster, 1992), 97.

94 Ibid., 82-83.

95 "Merriam-Webster Dictionary," Merriam-Webster, https://www.merriamwebster.com/ dictionary/anthropic%20principle (accessed June 13, 2019).

96 Chuck Missler, *Beyond Coincidence* (Coeur d'Alene, ID: Koinonia House, 2016), 456, Kindle Edition.

97 Ibid., 477, Kindle Edition.

98 Craig A. Perman, "Atoms and God's Order in the Fundamental Building Blocks of All Substance," Creation Ministries International, https://creation.com/atoms-and-gods-order (accessed June 13, 2019).

99 Gerard J. Keane, *Creation Rediscovered: Evolution and the Importance of the Origins Debate* (Charlotte, NC:

TAN Books, 1999), under "Chapter 8: Entropy," https://www.hoopladigital.com/play/ 12065628.

100 Calle, 73.

101 Ibid.

102 Alok Jha, "What Is the Second Law of Thermodynamics?" The Guardian, https://www.theguardian.com/science/2013/dec/01/what-is-the-second-law-of-thermodynamics (accessed October 13, 2019).

103 Missler, *Beyond Coincidence*, 580, Kindle Edition.

104 Oliver Burkeman, "Why Can't the World's Greatest Minds Solve the Mystery of Consciousness?" The Guardian, https://www.theguardian.com/science/2015/jan/21/-sp-why-cant-worlds-greatest-minds-solve-mystery-consciousness (accessed June 14, 2019).

105 Haisch, 50-51.

106 Lisa Miller, "Beyond Death: The Science of the Afterlife," Time, April 20, 2014, https://time.com/68381/life-beyond-death-the-science-of-the-afterlife-2/ (accessed July 8, 2019).

107 Ibid.

108 Ibid.

109 Haisch, 128.

110 Ibid., 131.

111 Rusty Leonard, "Base Royalties," World Magazine, December 5, 2009, https://world.wng.org/ 2009/11/base_royalties (accessed June 14, 2019).

112 Robert Laura, "Pastor Rick Warren Is Well Prepared for a Purpose Driven Retirement," Forbes, https://www.forbes.

com/sites/robertlaura/2013/03/21/pastor-rick-warren-is-practicing-what-he-preaches-and-getting-ready-for-retirement/#4d23c2524dbf (accessed June 14, 2019).

113 Davies, 16.

Chapter 6: The Digital 3-D Program Called "Life"

114 Musser, 45.

115 Jones and Robbins, 114.

116 Selbie, 30.

117 Ibid., 29.

118 Missler, *Beyond Perception*, 107, Kindle Edition.

119 Clara Moskowitz, "Are We Living in a Computer Simulation?" Scientific American, https://www.scientificamerican.com/article/are-we-living-in-a-computer-simulation/ (accessed June 19, 2019).

120 Olivia Solon, "Is our world a simulation? Why some scientists say it's more likely than not.," The Guardian, https://www.theguardian.com/technology/2016/oct/11/simulated-world-elon-musk-the-matrix (accessed June 19, 2019).

121 Missler, *Beyond Time & Space*, 971, Kindle Edition.

122 Clara Moskowitz, "Are We Living in a Computer Simulation?" Scientific American, https://www.scientificamerican.com/article/are-we-living-in-a-computer-simulation/ (accessed June 19, 2019).

123 Zetting, 157.

Chapter 7: Incoming Call from: GOD

124 Tim Burns, "Why Is the Bible, and Not Other Religious

Books, the Word of God?" The Christian Broadcasting Network, https://www1.cbn.com/spirituallife/the-word-of-god (accessed June 21, 2019).

125 Ibid.

126 Ibid.

127 Missler, *Beyond Time & Space*, 783, Kindle Edition.

128 Ralph O. Muncaster, *Can Archaeology Prove the Old Testament?* Examine the Evidence (Eugene, OR: Harvest House, 2000), 7.

129 Ibid.

130 A.J. Monty White, "The Piltdown Man Fraud," Creation Ministries International, https://creation.com/the-piltdown-man-fraud (accessed June 25, 2019).

131 Clifford and Barbara Wilson, *The Stones Still Shout: Sensational Highlights of the Bible and Archaeology,* 2nd ed. (Springfield, MO: Pacific International University, 2005), 17.

132 Ken Ham, "Geniuses, Not Brutes!" Answers in Genesis, https://answersingenesis.org/ archaeology/ancient-technology/geniuses-not-brutes/ (accessed June 25, 2019).

133 Wilson, *The Stones Still Shout*, 33.

134 Ibid, 43.

135 Andrew Lawler, "City of Biblical Abraham Brimmed with Trade and Riches," National Geographic. https://news.nationalgeographic.com/2016/03/160311-ur-iraq-trade-royal-cemetery-woolley-archaeology/ (accessed June 25, 2019).

136 Clifford Wilson, "Does Archaeology Support the Bible?" Answers in Genesis, https://answersingenesis.org/

archaeology/does-archaeology-support-the-bible/ (accessed June 26, 2019).

137 Chuck Missler, *Prophecy 2020: Profiling the Future through the Lens of Scripture* (Nashville, TN: Thomas Nelson, 2006), 29.

138 Wilson, *The Stones Still Shout*, 121.

139 Ibid., 128.

140 David Down, *The Archaeology Book*, Wonders of Creation (Green Forest, AR: Master Books, 2010), 35.

141 Ibid.

142 Paul E. Little, *Know Why You Believe* (Downers Grove, IL: InterVarsity Press, 2008), 110.

143 Clifford Wilson, "Does Archaeology Support the Bible?" Answers in Genesis, https://answersin genesis.org/archaeology/does-archaeology-support-the-bible/ (accessed June 26, 2019).

144 Sean McDowell, "What Is the Most Recent Manuscript Count for the New Testament?" Sean McDowell, https://seanmcdowell.org/blog/what-is-the-most-recent-manuscript-count-for-the-new-testament (accessed June 27, 2019).

145 "The Dead Sea Scrolls," The Israel Museum, Jerusalem, https://www.imj.org.il/en/ wings/shrine-book/dead-sea-scrolls (accessed June 27, 2019).

146 Josh McDowell, "Meticulous Scribe, Trusted Manuscript," Josh McDowell Ministry, https://www.josh.org/meticulous-scribes-trusted-manuscript/ (accessed June 27, 2019).

147 Ron Rhodes, "Manuscript Evidence for the Bible's

Reliability," Reasoning from the Scriptures Ministries, http://ronrhodes.org/articles/manuscript-evidence-for-the.html (accessed June 26, 2019).

148 Patrick Zukeran, "Historical Reliability of the Gospels," Evidence and Answers, https://evidenceandanswers.org/article/historical-reliability-of-the-gospels/ (accessed June 26, 2019).

149 Ibid., 617.

150 Little, 78.

151 John F. Walvoord, *Daniel: The Key to Prophetic Revelation* (Chicago: Moody Press, 1971), 17.

152 Dan Hayden, "Fulfilled Prophecy: Seven Compelling Evidences," Answers in Genesis, https://answersingenesis.org/is-the-bible-true/4-fulfilled-prophecy/ (accessed June 27, 2019).

153 Missler, *Beyond Coincidence*, 896-933, Kindle Edition.

154 Ibid., 1024.

155 Ibid.

156 R. A. Torrey, *What the Bible Teaches* (Peabody, MA: Hendrickson Publishers, Inc., 1998), 228.

157 Ibid., 229.

158 Charles Caldwell Ryrie, *Basic Theology* (Wheaton, IL: Victor Books, 1986), 325.

Chapter 8: Here, There, and Everywhere: The Multidimensionality of God

159 Trent C. Butler, ed., *Holman Bible Dictionary* (Nashville, TN: Holman Bible Publishers, 1991), under "Anthropomorphism," WORDsearch CROSS e-book.

160 Missler, *Beyond Perception,* 901-927, Kindle Edition.

161 Ibid.

162 Zetting, 23.

163 Ibid., 26.

164 Ibid., 27.

165 Selbie, 58.

166 Torrey, 4.

167 Ibid.

168 Ibid., 6.

169 Ibid., 13-14.

170 Acts 7:55-56.

171 John 16:7-10.

172 Torrey, 20.

173 Michael S. Heiser, *The Unseen Realm: Recovering the Supernatural Worldview of the Bible* (Bellingham, WA: Lexham Press, 2015), 63-65.

174 Ross, 97.

Chapter 9: Angels and Demons

175 Walter Martin and Ravi K. Zacharias, *The Kingdom of the Cults*, Revised and Updated Edition. (Minneapolis, MN: Bethany House Publishers, 2003), 436.

176 Ibid., 200.

177 Butler, ed., *Holman Bible Dictionary*, under "Angel," WORDsearch CROSS e-book.

178 William Evans, *The Great Doctrines of the Bible* (Chicago: Bible Institute Colportage Assoc., 1912), 216, WORDsearch CROSS e-book.

179 Robert B. Hughes and J. Carl Laney, *Tyndale Concise Bible Commentary* (Wheaton, IL: Tyndale House

Publishers, 1990), 12, WORDsearch CROSS e-book.

180 Ibid.

181 Butler, ed., *Holman Bible Dictionary,* under "Nephilim," WORDsearch CROSS e-book.

182 John MacArthur, *Macarthur New Testament Commentary* – 1 Peter (Chicago: Moody Press, 2004), 212, WORDsearch CROSS e-book.

183 Ibid., 213.

184 Hebrews 13:2.

185 Genesis 19:5, 10, 16.

186 Genesis 18:8; 19:3, 16.

187 Genesis 19, 2 Kings 19.

188 Chuck Missler, "Mischievous Angels or Sethites?" Koinonia House, http://www.khouse.org/ articles/1997/110/ (accessed May 27, 2019).

189 Strong, *Strong's Talking Greek and Hebrew Dictionary,* under "G746," WORDsearch CROSS e-book.

190 Ibid., under "G3613".

Chapter 10: Jesus: God in the Game

191 Strong, *Strong's Talking Greek and Hebrew Dictionary,* under "G5319," WORDsearch CROSS e-book.

192 John MacArthur, *Macarthur New Testament Commentary – Matthew 1-7* (Chicago: Moody Press, 1985), 16, WORDsearch CROSS e-book.

193 Granville, 108.

194 Willink, 163-64.

195 Ibid., 163.

196 Ibid., 165-66.

Chapter 11: Back to the Future: It's About Time!

197 Granville, 86-87.

198 Paul P. Enns, *Heaven Revealed: What Is It Like? What Will We Do?* (Chicago: Moody Publishers, 2011), 56.

199 Musser, 171.

200 Randy C. Alcorn, *Heaven* (Wheaton, IL: Tyndale House Publishers, 2004), 63.

201 Calle, 144.

202 Ibid., 145.

203 Ibid.

204 Arthur C. Custance, *Journey Out of Time* (Hamilton, ON, Canada: Doorway Publications, 2009), 37-38.

205 Ibid., 38.

206 Jones and Robbins, 277-78.

207 Custance, *Journey Out of Time*, 53.

208 Ibid., 10.

209 Missler, *Beyond Time and Space*, 786, Kindle Edition.

210 Arthur C. Custance, *Time and Eternity and Other Biblical Studies* (Grand Rapids, MI: Zondervan Publishing House, 1982), 43.

211 Ibid.

212 Alcorn, 250.

213 Granville, 106-7.

Chapter 12: Beam Me Up!

214 Ross, 137.

215 Steven J. Cole, "Entering God's Holy Presence" (sermon, Flagstaff Christian Fellowship, Flagstaff, AZ, July 8, 2018), https://bible.org/seriespage/20-entering-god-s-

holy-presence-exodus-401-38 (accessed July 25, 2019).

216 Ibid.

217 Tony Evans, *Victory in Spiritual Warfare* (Eugene, OR: Harvest House Publishers, 2011), 137.

Chapter 13: Fighting an Invisible Enemy

218 Strong, *Strong's Talking Greek and Hebrew*, under "G2032," WORDsearch CROSS e-book.

219 Evans, *Victory in Spiritual Warfare*, 18.

220 Ibid., 20.

221 Ibid., 21.

222 Strong, *Strong's Talking Greek and Hebrew Dictionary*, under "G3540," WORDsearch CROSS e-book.

223 Ibid.

224 Rick Warren, "The Battle for Your Mind" (sermon, Saddleback Church, Lake Forest, CA, October 1, 2010), https://www.desiringgod.org/messages/the-battle-for-your-mind (accessed August 6, 2019).

225 Evans, *Victory in Spiritual Warfare*, 34.

226 Evans, *Victory in Spiritual Warfare*, 64.

227 Ibid., 88.

228 Warren W. Wiersbe, *The Bible Exposition Commentary: New Testament Volume 2* (Wheaton, IL: Victor Books, 1989), 58.

229 John MacArthur, *MacArthur New Testament Commentary – Ephesians* (Chicago: Moody Press, 1986), 360, WORDsearch CROSS e-book.

230 Ibid., 371.

231 Ibid., 371.

Bibliography

Abbott, Edwin A. *Flatland: A Romance of Many Dimensions.* Mineola, NY: Dover Publications, 1992.

Aczel, Amir D. "Why Science Does Not Disprove God." Time, April 27, 2014. https://time.com/77676/why-science-does-not-disprove-god/ (accessed June 12, 2019).

Alcorn, Randy C. *Heaven.* Wheaton, IL: Tyndale House Publishers, 2004.

Bartolucci, Coby. "Dark Matter or Heavenly Matter?" The Odyssey Online, March 1, 2016. https://www.theodysseyonline.com/heavenly-matter-theory (accessed August 13, 2019).

Bradford, Barry. "Houdini's Greatest Trick – Debunking Fake Psychics." BarryBradford.com. http://barrybradford.com/houdini-greatest-trick/ (accessed June 6, 2019).

Burkeman, Oliver. "Why Can't the World's Greatest Minds Solve the Mystery of Consciousness?" The Guardian. https://www.theguardian.com/science/2015/jan/21/-sp-why-cant-worlds-greatest-minds-solve-mystery-consciousness (accessed June 14, 2019).

Burns, Tim. "Why Is the Bible, and Not Other Religious Books, the Word of God?" The Christian Broadcasting Network. https://www1.cbn.com/spirituallife/the-word-of-god (accessed June 21, 2019).

Butler, Trent C., ed. *Holman Bible Dictionary.* Nashville, TN: Holman Bible Publishers, 1991. WORDsearch CROSS e-book.

Calle, Carlos I. *Einstein for Dummies.* Hoboken, NJ: Wiley Publishing, 2005.

Cole, Steven J. "Entering God's Holy Presence." Sermon, Flagstaff Christian Fellowship, Flagstaff, AZ, July 8, 2018. https://bible.org/seriespage/20-entering-god-s-holy-presence-exodus-401-38 (accessed July 25, 2019).

Custance, Arthur C. *Journey Out of Time.* Hamilton, ON, Canada: Doorway Publications, 2009.

_____. *Time and Eternity and Other Biblical Studies.* Grand Rapids, MI: Zondervan Publishing House, 1982.

Davies, P. C. W. *The Mind of God: The Scientific Basis for a Rational World.* New York: Simon & Schuster, 1992.

Dolphin, Lambert. "The History of Hyperspace." Koinonia House. http://www.khouse.org/articles/1997/29/ (accessed June 5, 2019).

Down, David. *The Archaeology Book.* Wonders of Creation. Green Forest, AR: Master Books, 2010.

Edwards, Owen. "How Thomas Jefferson Created His Own Bible." Smithsonian.com. https://www.smithsonianmag.com/arts-culture/how-thomas-jefferson-created-his-own-bible-5659505/ (accessed May 25, 2019).

Enns, Paul P. *Heaven Revealed: What Is It Like? What Will We Do?* Chicago: Moody Publishers, 2011.

Evans, Tony. *Victory in Spiritual Warfare.* Eugene, OR: Harvest House Publishers, 2011.

Evans, William. *The Great Doctrines of the Bible.* Chicago: Bible Institute Colportage Assoc., 1912. WORDsearch CROSS e-book.

Gangel, Kenneth O., and Stephen J. Bramer. *Holman Old Testament Commentary – Genesis*. Edited by Max Anders. Nashville, TN: Broadman & Holman, 2003. WORDsearch CROSS e-book

Granville, William Anthony. *The Fourth Dimension and the Bible*. Boston: The Gotham Press, 1922.

Green, Emma. "A Lot of Americans Think the Spirit World Exists." The Atlantic, May 7, 2014. https://www.theatlantic.com/national/archive/2014/05/have-you-been-possessed-by-spirits/361680/ (accessed May 24, 2019).

Haisch, Bernard. *The God Theory: Universes, Zero-Point Fields and What's Behind It All*. San Francisco, CA: Weiser Books, 2006.

Halpern, Paul. *The Great Beyond: Higher Dimensions, Parallel Universes and the Extraordinary Search for a Theory of Everything*. Hoboken, NJ: J. Wiley, 2004.

_____. "Spiritual Hyperplane: How Spiritualists of the 19th Century Forged a Lasting Association between Higher Dimensions and the Occult World." Aeon. https://aeon.co/essays/the-occult-roots-of-higher-dimensional-research-in-physics (accessed June 5, 2019).

Ham, Ken. "Geniuses, Not Brutes!" Answers in Genesis. https://answersingenesis.org/archaeology/ancient-technology/geniuses-not-brutes/ (accessed June 25, 2019).

_____. "What Was God Doing Before Creation?" Answers in Genesis.

https://answersingenesis.org/answers/biblical-authority-devotional/where-does-god-live/what-was-god-doing-before-creation/ (accessed May 27, 2019).

Hayden, Dan. "Fulfilled Prophecy: Seven Compelling Evidences." Answers in Genesis. https://answersingenesis.org/is-the-bible-true/4-fulfilled-prophecy/ (accessed June 27, 2019).

Heiser, Michael S. *Supernatural*. Bellingham, WA: Lexham Press, 2015.

_____. *The Unseen Realm: Recovering the Supernatural Worldview of the Bible*. Bellingham, WA: Lexham Press, 2015.

Hughes, Robert B., and J. Carl Laney. *Tyndale Concise Bible Commentary*. Wheaton, IL: Tyndale House Publishers, 1990. WORDsearch CROSS e-book.

Izlar, Kelly. "Atomic Flashback: A Century of the Bohr Model." CERN. https://home.cern/news/news/physics/atomic-flashback-century-bohr-model (accessed October 13, 2019).

Jha, Alok. "What Is the Second Law of Thermodynamics?" The Guardian. https://www.theguardian.com/science/2013/dec/01/what-is-the-second-law-of-thermodynamics (accessed October 13, 2019).

Jones, Andrew Zimmerman, and Daniel Robbins. *String Theory for Dummies*. Hoboken, NJ: Wiley Publishers, 2010.

Kaiser, Walter C. *Hard Sayings of the Bible*. Downers Grove, IL: InterVarsity Press, 1996. WORDsearch CROSS e-book.

Keane, Gerard J. *Creation Rediscovered: Evolution and the Importance of the Origins Debate*. Charlotte, NC: TAN Books, 1999. https://www.hoopladigital.com/play/12065628.

Kestin, Greg. "What Does an Atom Look Like?" PBS. https://www.pbs.org/wgbh/nova/video/what-does-an-atom-look-like/ (June 9, 2019).

Laura, Robert. "Pastor Rick Warren Is Well Prepared for a Purpose Driven Retirement." Forbes. https://www.forbes.com/sites/robertlaura/2013/03/21/pastor-rick-warren-is-practicing-what-he-preaches-and-getting-ready-for-retirement/#4d23c2524dbf (accessed June 14, 2019).

Lawler, Andrew. "City of Biblical Abraham Brimmed with Trade and Riches." National Geographic. https://news.nationalgeographic.com/2016/03/160311-ur-iraq-trade-royal-cemetery-woolley-archaeology/ (accessed June 25, 2019).

Leonard, Rusty "Base Royalties," World Magazine, December 5, 2009. https://world.wng.org/2009/11/base_royalties (accessed June 14, 2019).

Little, Paul E. *Know Why You Believe*. Downers Grove, IL: InterVarsity Press, 2008.

MacArthur, John. *Macarthur New Testament Commentary – 1 Peter*. Chicago: Moody Press, 2004. WORDsearch CROSS e-book.

_____. *Macarthur New Testament Commentary – Ephesians*. Chicago: Moody Press, 1986. WORDsearch CROSS e-book.

_____. *Macarthur New Testament Commentary – Matthew 1-7*. Chicago: Moody Press, 1985. WORDsearch CROSS e-book.

Mariani, Mike. "American Exorcism." The Atlantic, December 2018. https://www.theatlantic.com/magazine/archive/2018/12/catholic-exorcisms-on-the-rise/573943/ (accessed May 24, 2019).

Martin, Walter, and Ravi K. Zacharias. *The Kingdom of the Cults*. Revised and Updated Edition. Minneapolis, MN: Bethany House Publishers, 2003.

Mauk, Ben. "Where Do Electrons Get Energy to Spin Around an Atom's Nucleus?" Live Science. https://www.livescience.com/32427-where-do-electrons-get-energy-to-spin-around-an-atoms-nucleus.html (Accessed June 9, 2019).

McDowell, Josh. "Meticulous Scribe, Trusted Manuscript." Josh McDowell Ministry. https://www.josh.org/meticulous-scribes-trusted-manuscript/ (accessed June 27, 2019).

McDowell, Sean. "What Is the Most Recent Manuscript Count for the New Testament?" Sean McDowell. https://seanmcdowell.org/blog/what-is-the-most-recent-manuscript-count-for-the-new-testament (accessed June 27, 2019).

McMullen, Chris Ph.D. *The Visual Guide to Extra Dimensions*. Vol. 1. N.p.: Custom Books, 2008.

"Merriam-Webster Dictionary." Merriam-Webster. https://www.merriam-webster.com/dictionary/anthropic%20principle (accessed June 13, 2019).

Miller, Lisa "Beyond Death: The Science of the Afterlife," Time, April 20, 2014, https://time.com/68381/life-beyond-death-the-science-of-the-afterlife-2/ (accessed July 8, 2019).

Missler, Chuck. *Beyond Coincidence.* Coeur d'Alene, ID: Koinonia House, 2016. Kindle Edition.

_____. *Beyond Newton.* Coeur d'Alene, ID: Koinonia House, 2016. Kindle Edition.

_____. *Beyond Perception.* Coeur d'Alene, ID: Koinonia House, 2016. Kindle Edition.

_____. *Beyond Time & Space.* Coeur d'Alene, ID: Koinonia House, 2016. Kindle Edition.

_____. "Mischievous Angels or Sethites?" Koinonia House. http://www.khouse.org/ articles/1997/110/ (accessed May 27, 2019).

_____. *Prophecy 2020: Profiling the Future through the Lens of Scripture.* Nashville, TN: Thomas Nelson, 2006.

Moskowitz, Clara. "Are We Living in a Computer Simulation?" Scientific American. https://www.scientificamerican.com/article/are-we-living-in-a-computer-simulation/ (accessed June 19, 2019).

Muncaster, Ralph O. *Can Archaeology Prove the Old Testament?* Examine the Evidence. Eugene, OR: Harvest House, 2000.

Musser, George. *The Complete Idiot's Guide to String Theory.* New York: Alpha, 2008.

Perman, Craig A. "Atoms and God's Order in the Fundamental Building Blocks of All Substance." Creation Ministries

International. https://creation.com/atoms-and-gods-order (accessed June 13, 2019).

Redd, Nola Taylor. "What Is Dark Matter?" Space.com. https://www.space.com/20930-dark-matter.html (accessed August 13, 2019).

Rhodes, Ron. "Manuscript Evidence for the Bible's Reliability." Reasoning from the Scriptures Ministries. http://ronrhodes.org/articles/manuscript-evidence-for-the.html (accessed June 26, 2019).

Rock, Meghan. String Theory. Great Discoveries in Science. New York: Cavendish Square Publishing, 2017. https://www.hoopladigital.com/play/12171869 (accessed June 14, 2019).

Ross, Hugh. *Beyond the Cosmos: The Extra-Dimensionality of God*. 2nd ed. Colorado Springs, CO: NavPress, 1999.

Rucker, Rudy v. B. *Geometry, Relativity, and the Fourth Dimension*. New York: Dover Publications, 1977.

Ryrie, Charles Caldwell. *Basic Theology*. Wheaton, IL: Victor Books, 1986.

Selbie, Joseph. *The Physics of God: Unifying Quantum Physics, Consciousness, M-Theory, Heaven, Neuroscience, and Transcendence*. Wayne, NJ: New Page Books/Career Press, 2018.

Solon, Olivia. "Is our world a simulation? Why some scientists say it's more likely than not." The Guardian. https://www.theguardian.com/technology/2016/oct/11/simulated-world-elon-musk-the-matrix (accessed June 19, 2019).

"Stories of Joplin: The Spook Light." Joplin Missouri Official Website. https://www.joplinmo.org/575/The-Spook-Light (accessed November 10, 2019).

Strong, James. *Strong's Talking Greek and Hebrew Dictionary*. Austin, TX: WORDsearch Corp., 2007. WORDsearch CROSS e-book.

"The Dead Sea Scrolls." The Israel Museum, Jerusalem. https://www.imj.org.il/en/wings/shrine-book/dead-sea-scrolls (accessed June 27, 2019).

Torrey, R. A. *What the Bible Teaches*. Peabody, MA: Hendrickson Publishers, Inc., 1998.

Walvoord, John F. *Daniel: The Key to Prophetic Revelation*. Chicago: Moody Press, 1971.

Warren, Rick. "The Battle for Your Mind." Sermon, Saddleback Church, Lake Forest, CA, October 1, 2010. https://www.desiringgod.org/messages/the-battle-for-your-mind (accessed August 6, 2019).

White, A.J. Monty. "The Piltdown Man Fraud." Creation Ministries International. https://creation.com/the-piltdown-man-fraud (accessed June 25, 2019).

Wiersbe, Warren W. *The Bible Exposition Commentary: New Testament Volume 2*. Wheaton, IL: Victor Books, 1989.

Willink, Arthur. *The World of the Unseen*. London: MacMillan and Co., 1893.

Wilson, Clifford. "Does Archaeology Support the Bible?" Answers in Genesis. https://answersingenesis.org/archaeology/does-archaeology-support-the-bible/ (accessed June 26, 2019).

Wilson, Clifford and Barbara. *The Stones Still Shout: Sensational Highlights of the Bible and Archaeology.* 2nd ed. Springfield, MO: Pacific International University, 2005

Wormald, Benjamin. "Scientists and Belief." Pew Research Center. https://www.pewforum.org/2009/11/05/scientists-and-belief/ (accessed June 11, 2019).

Zetting, Dennis. *A Quantum Case for God.* Lynden, WA: Quantum Creation Ministries, 2016.

Zukeran, Patrick. "Historical Reliability of the Gospels." Evidence and Answers. https://evidenceandanswers.org/article/historical-reliability-of-the-gospels/ (accessed June 26, 2019).